What people are saying about Cracking Up...

*"What a humble, insightful portrait of addiction and recovery. So many powerful truths that shatter the vices of denial and dispel family myths. **Cracking Up** is a must-read for those who seek release from the pain and effects of addictive, destructive lifestyles. Blessings to Dr. J. and Rudy for having the courage to share their journey. It's destined to open the doors to a healing balm that transforms lives."*

Shellye L. Sledge, MSW, ACSW - Executive Director
P O W E R - Positive Opportunities for Women, Youth and Families Engaged in Recovery
San Diego, CA

---

*"To face one's demons is as difficult as it is liberating. In **Cracking Up** mother (co-dependent) and son (ex-addict) bare their souls with such poignant honesty that the reader comes to understand well their personal price for freedom. Their story, told raw and unabashed, holds life lessons for all families attempting to slay the addiction monster. It is a tale of redemption, a gift of hope."*

La Mar Hasbrouck, MD
Adjunct Clinical Professor, Morehouse School of Medicine
Atlanta, GA

---

*"This is a masterful and sensitive account of a mother and son's battle with the devastating effects of drug and alcohol addiction. The book's unique dual voice underscores the stark reality of addiction, dependence, and survival. I highly recommend **Cracking Up**."*

Robert V. Guthrie, Ph.D.
Professor Emeritus of Psychology
San Diego, CA

---

*"**Cracking Up** is an extraordinarily honest and profound guide. Not only does it open the door to understanding the horrific grip of addiction, it also provides a significant step-by-step plan for recovery, hope, and relief. Dr. Lorraine and Rudolph Johnson have developed a remarkable remedy that's designed to heal the mind, strengthen the body, and comfort the soul."*

Dr. Grace Cornish
Author of: *You Deserve Healthy Love, Sis!*
New York

CRACKING UP

**The true story of
one family's recovery
from the devastation
of crack cocaine**

CRACKING UP

**The true story of
one family's recovery
from the devastation
of crack cocaine**

Written by mother and son

Lorraine R. Johnson Ph.D., L.C.S.W.

and

Rudolph A. Johnson III

MOSLEY
PUBLISHING
GROUP

www.mosleypublishing.com

A Piece of
Blackberry Pie, Inc.
FOOD 4 THOUGHT

crackingupthebook@cox.net

A Piece of Blackberry Pie, Inc. and
Mosley Publishing Group
San Diego, California

Editing by Karen L. Wilkening, Expert Editing, Ink.
Cover, Layout and Graphics by Stacy Hodge, PD Graphics
Cover photo by Robert Fortson

ISBN 1886185-03-4
1st printing, October 2003
Printed in the U.S.A.

DEDICATIONS

I dedicate this book to God,
who gave me the spiritual vision for this project.

To my father Frank H. Barnes Sr.,
who battled all his life with alcohol and drugs until it finally killed him.
To my family, who encouraged me to write this story
and gave me the confidence to tell the truth.

To my children who inherited a genetic predisposition to alcohol and drugs:
My son Rudy for his inspiration, spirit, and willingness
to tell his story with mine;
My son Randy, who still struggles towards sobriety:
God has an awesome ministry for you;
My son Rashad, committed to saying "no" to alcohol and drugs
and "yes" to life.

To my deceased husband, Andrew Earl Thompson Sr., my personal angel.

And to the memory of my best sister-friend Becky:
I know you have found eternal peace with the Creator.

To all the families and friends of alcoholics and addicts:
May our story help you have faith and hope in the recovery process.
Let us go in search of our lost family members
and help them into the healing zone.

Dr. Lorraine R. Johnson

I'd like to dedicate this book to Sheryl, my wife of 14 years,
and to our wonderful children, Rudy IV and Mallory.
They are the force behind my burning desire to stay sober,
one day at a time.

Most of all, to those
who are still struggling with their addictions.

Rudolph A. Johnson III

CONTENTS

ACKNOWLEDGMENTS

My sincerest thanks to...
My mother and father, Frank H. Barnes Sr.
and Lovolia Davis, who gave me life;
My grandmother, "Nana," for believing I could do anything I set my mind to;
My siblings, brother Frank H. Barnes Jr. and sisters Lavon Davis,
Australia Tucker, and "sister-daughter," Markay McKinney,
for their unconditional support and love;
My sons Rudolph, Randolph, and Rashad, and their father, Rudolph A. Johnson, Jr.,
for all the heartfelt lessons I've learned through you.

My business partner and spiritual sister, Dr. Carol Williams; My best friend and
soul-mate Tony Lamar, who understands all my gifts and faults and remains one of
my best supporters; My "best-est" friend in the world, Barbara Gunner,
for being there for me through the entire writing process.

My lovely daughters-in-law, Sheryl and Javette, for loving and
supporting my sons and for giving me the greatest gift of all,
my grandchildren Rudolph IV, Nia, and Mallory.

To Grandma Ruth, our angel guide; Albert Noone, my nephew-son who
conducts a live-in prison ministry; Joseph Waheed, my God-brother and
co-parent; Ruth E. Johnson-Aaron, who continues to be my spiritual sister and
intellectual mentor; Trudye Johnson, my other dear sister; Lottie Perkins,
a visionary who saw the book coming long before we did; and my
neighbor-sister-friend Alyse Allen, who allowed me the space to cry,
laugh and fall apart whenever I needed to.

My sister-in-law, Mary Barnes, who always supports me in everything I attempt to do;
Ellis Porter, a true friend always willing to listen to my pain and joy;
and Patrick McKinney, who is like a son to me.

Many thanks also to Bob, who told me I should write; to our editor Karen Louise,
for her sensitivity and "Expert Editing" touch; to Stacy Hodge of PD Graphics
for her outstanding book design; and to Deborah Mosley of
Mosley Publishing Group, who is an angel.
Thank you all for helping us transform this dream into a reality.

Dr. Lorraine R. Johnson

ACKNOWLEDGMENTS

First and foremost I'd like to thank my
Higher Power, whom I like to call "God,"
for helping me to humble myself enough to write this book.

I wish to thank my wife and life-long partner, Sheryl Mallory-Johnson,
who is truly my rock. She has cared for me through the good
and bad times of our friendship.
To my children, Rudy IV and Mallory – I thank you being patient with Daddy.
I also want to thank my writing partner, my Mother.
It is a joy to watch this project come to fruition together.

Both my Mom and I want to thank Karen, our editor, and
Deborah and her publishing team for their assistance along the way.

Thanks also to the players and coaching staff of Texas Southern University
for saving a young man like me.
Finally, I want to thank those addicts/alcoholics out there
for their trust and belief in me.

Rudolph A. Johnson III

PREFACE

Dr. Lorraine R. Johnson

The inspiration to write this book came from a dream I had a number of years ago. My Higher Power, whom I call God, came to me in this dream and informed me that my son and I would write a recovery book together and call it *Cracking Up*. When I called Rudy to tell him about it, he said that God had given him the same spiritual idea. It was then I realized the dream was a call to a new ministry. It has been a long journey of patience and surrender to the will of Higher Power, but this book is the first fruit. I pray that this very personal story of our struggle and triumph through Rudy's addiction, my enabling and co-dependency, and our family's cracking up will be insightful and useful.

May you and your family, friends, students and organizations be as blessed and healed as we have been by the God-given experience of creating this book for you.

Rudolph A. Johnson III

It has taken over ten years of sobriety to prepare myself to write about the massive destruction of my illness of alcoholism and drug addiction. It's a difficult task to put such personal thoughts and embarrassing truths on paper. But I'm compelled to tell my story, alongside my mother's, because I believe it will be helpful for others to read about making it through substance abuse to sobriety.

My hope is that my story of pain and struggle will exemplify one's ability to take action to overcome the hurdles and obstacles of "getting on the other side" and putting a shattered life back together. I am willing to bare my soul with still-struggling alcoholics and addicts, their co-dependents, family members, friends and anyone who needs a ray of hope that change is possible. I pray you do not give up before your miracle happens.

CHAPTER I

MOTHER: MY BABY

SON: GROWING UP HIGH

MOTHER: MY BABY

It seems like yesterday that I was 20 years old, in love, married to my childhood sweetheart and anxiously awaiting the birth of our first child. As the wife of a man in the US Air Force, I was able to travel to many places I had never been, and Anchorage, Alaska was where we were stationed at the time.

I was so excited to realize that my childhood dream for a family was finally taking shape. I frequently fantasized about what my child would be like, how I would raise him, how he would never want for anything, and most importantly, how perfect his life would be.

On the night that I went into labor my hopes seemed to be shattered. My labor was hard, the delivery was very difficult, and the baby was in trouble.

When Rudolph Allister Johnson III was finally born he was in immediate danger. He had remained in the birthing canal position for too long and as a result he was covered with a thin layer of bluish white skin from head to toe. His head was very oblong and his breathing was shallow. The doctors raced him to the pediatric intensive care unit. They placed him into an incubator, where he was administered oxygen and fed antibiotics intravenously.

Shortly afterward a priest came to my room and said, "Your son Rudy has experienced a lack of oxygen and possible poisoning from amniotic fluid. The doctors are doing all they can, but they do not expect him to make it through the night."

My husband and I were devastated, as this was something beyond the imaginable. My body was trying to recover from giving birth, and my soul was shattered from the inside out by this unexpected and horrible news. We prayed all night long and even though we did not sleep, we made it through. Early the next morning we were informed that Rudy was still struggling to stay alive but that we could visit him in the infant critical care unit.

I was shocked by my baby son's physical appearance. He was in isolation with several tubes inserted into his tiny arms and nose. Although I could not hold him, my heart immediately went out to him and we instantly bonded. I held on tightly to him in my spirit, embraced his very essence, and prayed very hard.

Each day against medical staff's expectations, "Baby Rudy" improved, displaying an incredibly strong will to live. By the end of his first two weeks of life he was breathing on his own and had begun eating. His skin went from that frightening bluish-white to a rich chocolate brown.

Yet even with all the miraculous occurrences and despite the fact that Rudy appeared to be progressing very well, the doctor told us, "Your son might experience mild to severe brain damage due to the lack of oxygen during labor." Once again we were devastated, but remained hopeful, faithful and positive. I wiped out any negative thoughts from my mind and refused to claim any of it.

Over the next few years, Rudy, through the grace of God, began to develop into a very bright, curious, intelligent young infant and toddler. He proved he was more than a survivor – there was no evidence of brain damage.

When Rudy was three, my husband left the Air Force and we came back home to live in San Diego, California. We lived in a small apartment in the inner city (31st Street) and we both worked full-time jobs while pursuing our college educations. Our ultimate dream was to obtain advanced degrees and move our sons from the inner city to our dream house. And to live happily ever after, of course.

By the time he was in the second grade, Rudy was identified as gifted and was placed in an advanced education program for exceptional students.

As a parent, I was on a mission to give Rudy everything I did not have and in general make sure his life was better than mine. I resolved he would have nothing but the best and would not have to deal with the harsh realities that I had faced. Especially since Rudy was my firstborn, I had very high expectations for him. I expected Rudy to be better than I ever was. I wanted a fantasy child, the perfect child. My child would talk and walk early, potty train quickly, be well-mannered, independent and a little superstar.

My hopes and expectations weren't meant to be in any way emotionally stressful for Rudy: They were to ensure that he would never experience the emotional pain, rejection or low self esteem that I had to work through. I considered him my little miracle child and was sure that he would get high academic marks, attend college, invent something worthwhile for mankind and achieve his highest goals.

Even though I was consumed with making the perfect family life for Rudy, somehow I failed to realize the possible effects of things going on around us, and in our house. From a young age Rudy was exposed to family and friends who indulged in recreational drugs. A "survivor of the 60's," I was oblivious to the long-term effects of drug use.

I thought a "normal" exposure would give him a protective, realistic peek at life in the fast lane and he would have what is referred to as a

"Ph.D. in the street." After all, my grandmother always told me, "Don't be an educated fool." To me that meant to learn something from life itself, not just books. I thought my precocious son could have knowledge of what was happening on the streets, but at the same time not let it touch him.

In those days there was very little educational information available on the long-term affects of substance abuse. It was the age of drug experimentation. The norm in my community was that having a few drinks or smoking marijuana was cool, and it was not a big deal to snort a line or two of cocaine for fun or relaxation. There were no drugs around like there are now, designer drugs and heroin. We just thought everybody was snorting a few lines and smoking some dope (marijuana), drinking malt liquor or other alcohol, and when they didn't want to do it anymore – they didn't have to.

The people in our circle of family and friends were not being dysfunctional, stealing, or losing their jobs or houses. We didn't see it as a disease. And I for one was oblivious to the seriousness of using alcohol and recreational drugs. Though I never encouraged Rudy to use any of these substances, he was exposed to family and friends at parties who regularly drank alcohol and used different drugs. My husband also openly smoked marijuana in our home and I saw nothing wrong with it. He was a functional individual who was responsible for his family, and in his community.

While my husband and some of our family and friends participated in recreational drug use, I was always able to set boundaries and say, "No, thanks." I also thought my children would be able to do the same.

I was sure that if I established a foundation for Rudy that was grounded in God, he would stay on the straight and narrow. So Sunday school was very important to me and was a regular ritual for our family. This way, I thought that Rudy would excel, be blessed and spared from any emotional or traumatic experiences. What I did not think about was that I was powerless to outcomes, and that Rudy would have to experience life on life's unpredictable terms. I forgot that I could give birth, but not life. I forgot that I could give only guidance and not guarantees. I truly believed that if I followed my little "recipe" on how to have the perfect child, that Rudy would grow into a healthy, productive, successful adult.

In junior high school Rudy again exceeded our expectations. Counselors, teachers and relatives were impressed with his academic achievement and also spoke highly of his personality. He was very adapted. Never did I worry that he was experiencing traumatic growing pains or emotional stress. I would stand in the shadows and beam at his development and special accomplishments. I did not think that Rudy was better than anyone else, but I certainly was appreciative and proud to see that he was an above-average young man. He always seemed to rise to the occasion and to excel. Nothing seemed too much for him to handle. In grade school and junior high I saw him as very well adjusted, social and able to get along with both his peers and adults.

Rudy graduated from ninth grade and entered high school. By this time, I felt that I had exposed him to enough academic, social and real life experiences that would equip him to make healthy, good, solid decisions. He immediately tried out and made his high school varsity football team. As the quarterback, Rudy once again snagged a starring role. He led his team to many victories and encouraged them through the agony of defeat.

As I watched him master his leadership role, I knew Rudy was a winner and leader. He graduated from high school with high academic marks and was sought after by several colleges. He was offered and accepted a four-year academic and athletic scholarship from Texas Southern University in Houston, Texas. Again, his accomplishments were the buzzwords in our house. I was so proud and happy for Rudy's success, and the realization of my dreams for him.

That summer, we began to plan and shop for his upcoming departure for college and excitement rang in the air. The day before he left, we had a huge family potluck and celebration. The whole family was very proud of Rudy's accomplishments. The next morning I took Rudy to the airport for his trip to Texas. During the drive, I had mixed emotions. I was overjoyed that my firstborn would have the opportunity to attend a renowned African-American university, partially because I had always wanted to do so myself but didn't have the grades or resources when I got out of high school.

Texas Southern would challenge him academically, reinforce his culture, facilitate his spiritual development and treat him like a "true" extended family member. From my perspective Rudy was not only intellectually prepared, he was also ahead of the "pack" emotionally, spiritually, experientially and physically. He had earned a full four-year athletic and academic scholarship. During his pre-college visits, he expressed excitement and seemed very happy with his decision to attend Texas Southern University even though this was to be his first time living in another state, away from home, completely on his own.

I remember looking at him with such pride. I thought my heart would literally jump out of my chest. I was excited like a little girl experiencing her first Christmas and Santa had left every toy on her wish list. I could hardly contain myself. It was as if I was the 18-year old going off to the college of my choice, seeking knowledge, exciting adventures and personal success. I may have been so caught up in reliving my own personal adventures and dreams, that I didn't have a clue as to what Rudy III was feeling, thinking or dealing with. I was so absorbed with projecting his hopes and dreams that I was oblivious to Rudy's reality. My brave, successful son did not show me the slightest qualms about leaving home.

I was so excited that I was in rare form the day he left home. I made sure he had everything I wanted him to have, packed and ready to go. During the weeks leading up to this day, I had even coordinated a family support system in Texas.

As I rushed him to the airport, I chatted idly until it was time for him to board his plane, kissed him on the cheek, made sure he had ample personal spending money, hugged him tight and pushed him onto the boarding line. I stayed until the plane became airborne and totally out of sight. He was on his way to another successful adventure. All was well in my soul that day.

As I sit here today and write, I wrack my brain to see if I can conjure up any hint, any sign at all that on that day my man-child, my African King, my hero, my genius, my baby, was addicted to crack cocaine.

SON: GROWING UP HIGH

I vividly recall the ingenuity we had as children playing sports, our creative minds rising to the challenge of limited surroundings. Although we lived in poverty-stricken communities with barren schoolyards, broken-down playgrounds, neglected recreational centers, glass-infested alleys, pothole-ridden streets, and little to no parental supervision, this was our neighborhood and in spite of it all, we took great pride in it. We managed to dream beyond our limited environment and make the best of what our Higher Power provided.

Our baseball diamond consisted of a vacant lot with concrete walkways and an old abandoned garage. It was on this makeshift diamond that we played seasons of baseball games. I still recall those steel trashcan lids used as base pads, creating the "invisible man" concept to assist us with ghost base-running, our forced-out rule, and some pre-measured homerun fences to accommodate our youthful strength.

Our football gridiron was the front lawn of my grandmother's house, which was literally just a few doors down from the apartment where I lived with my mother, father and brother Randy. It's strange, but I still claim that small piece of grassy area, with a concrete strip down the middle, as the training ground that paid for my college education. We played on that front lawn into the wee hours of the night. The concrete strip down the middle was live, and one could be tackled on that strip if he was not careful. And the end zone was a solid brick wall that we had to jump over as we reached scoring position.

We also played basketball in the common area in back. It wasn't a backyard per se, but one big yard within the apartment complex that we all shared. We simply cut the bottom out of one of those old plastic trashcans, large enough for a basketball to fit through, and hung it from some wooden stilts that we nailed to the top of the roof. We used chalk to mark out the key as well as the half-court boundaries. Our innovation and creativity was born in these surroundings.

I personally take pride in being a product of that culture of children who came out of the neighborhood. But we quickly found other ways to provide ourselves with entertainment, and the childish innocence of these homemade street games did not last.

Growing up "high" on or under the influence of a substance was commonplace for me. Our apartment was located on 31st Street and Ocean View Boulevard in San Diego, California. This area, in retrospect, was aesthetically terrible, an armpit of San Diego society. But back then it was all we knew. It was our home and it included alcoholics, winos, addicts and all the other cool individuals hanging out in the neighborhood. At that time, no one used the words addict or alcoholic. No one was overly cautious around them, nor did anyone call the police or law enforcement. They were simply part of the community – neither good nor bad – just reality.

I remember that I had vowed not to be one of those individuals on skid row begging for a dollar and a quarter to buy cheap wine from the corner liquor store. That was something I didn't want to turn into. As the oldest of three brothers, I was responsible and independent from a very young age. I didn't relate to people on what we called hard drugs, like heroin, or to those people we figured were schizophrenic, mentally distressed, or just plain crazy.

Back in those days I hung out with a group of four guys who were very close to me. Our clique was made up of a combination of family and friends. We knew we would not end up like the guys who were drunk with a cigarette hanging out of their mouths or a joint rolled up between their lips. But being macho and cool back then was all about how many beers you could drink, how many joints you could smoke, how many lines you could toot. We were destined for the inevitable. Yet we thought that occupying ourselves with other activities like sports would make us less susceptible to using alcohol and drugs.

Family get-togethers were big. All the family members, young to old, would attend. Drinking and marijuana smoking were rampant at these gatherings. It was nothing to go to a dark corner of the house and find someone tooting a line of cocaine. It was actually expected from those providing the entertainment. It was commonplace. In fact it was the norm.

As a result, the children in my neighborhood looked at their parents, aunts, uncles, cousins, nieces, nephews, godfathers and everyone indulging in that kind of activity, and began emulating that behavior. We soon evolved into having our own little ritual of getting high and "doing our thing" at our own get-togethers.

My very first experience with marijuana is foggy, but I do remember that it occurred somewhere between my seventh and eighth birthdays. By the time I was ten or eleven my buddies and I were sneaking joints – going in the back, lighting up and passing them around. It was fun and games with no consequences.

One thing led to another and the next substance I experimented with was alcohol. We started sneaking beers when I was thirteen years old. And then a daily pattern of pot smoking evolved. Waking up and having a joint in the morning was as commonplace to us as having a cup of coffee and reading the newspaper was to most people. When smoking pot in the morning became a regular event, things got trickier. The drug use itself was not as scary as the hoops I had to jump through to get the drugs. I wasn't old enough to earn money, so I had to save and scrape enough together in order to get high.

Marijuana was definitely the in thing for our particular group in high school. It wasn't so much the hard drugs or the alcohol in those years: Marijuana was bigger and better to get high on. From the tenth grade to my senior year, I was smoking weed with my friends three or four times a day. It began taking over my life and controlling my every move, but I was adept at covering it up.

Ironically, I was still bringing home grades of A's and B's from school. To continue performing in the classroom was part of my cover-up. I felt that as long as I brought home good grades, no one was the wiser. Another positive in my life was athletics. Football was always my baseline and my love for the sport continued to grow. Ever since I was a child, playing sports kept me sane, in my right mind. Going to practice every day helped keep me in good shape and encouraged me to keep my grades up in order to continue playing sports. Football was my Love Jones. If I could not play, I was nothing. I didn't want to stop. That is what kept me on the edge until my senior year in high school.

During my senior year an acquaintance of mine turned me, and a good friend, onto the powder form of cocaine. It was so new and such a taboo to us. But we felt we were indestructible. We had the community and the leadership of the school in the palm of our hands because we were ball players and had turned our team from losers to victors that year. We were really walking on air, riding high. And getting high on cocaine.

Then we graduated to rock (crack) cocaine. The sensation from this drug was euphoric – an indescribable rush that is felt throughout your body. I immediately knew that I preferred this drug to every other substance I had ever tried. By the time I graduated from high school, I had gotten high on crack about three or four times.

In retrospect, it's plain to see that our twelfth grade year as student athletes had spun out of control, but we got away with it because we stayed functional. Drug use was a daily experience. A group of about four of us would trade off the responsibility of obtaining the marijuana sack for that day, whether it was a five, ten or even a twenty-dollar bag. At our age it was difficult to continuously come up with that kind of money, but we were not tempted to steal for it. The money we used for drugs was food and entertainment allowances given from home. We skipped meals and saved up in order to have the funds to buy marijuana.

As a result of getting high we sometimes neglected our class time because we couldn't come to class with red, tight eyes and reeking of marijuana. Skipping one class often meant skipping the rest of the day to allow ourselves to become functional again. But we had it down pat. We knew exactly which classes we could skip without much of an excuse. We even knew how long it would take to come down off any particular high.

Our after-school activity would basically be the four of us getting together and having a big smoke-out to see who could roll the largest joint, who could smoke the biggest joint, and who could outlast who.

When I thought ahead, I figured that once I got to college I could alleviate my need for drugs and begin with a clean slate.

Well, one day we received good news. Two of the four of us where awarded four-year scholarships to Texas Southern University. The TSU athletic director had been in San Diego doing some recruiting. He had interviewed various people around the city, asking who would be interested in coming to a predominantly black college and playing a little football.

At that time, my father was the President and CEO of the San Diego Urban League. The athletic director stopped by to see my father, not knowing, of course, that he was my dad. He asked my dad to point him in the direction of some young African-American athletics who were pretty good students with good heads on their shoulders and willing to study at a black university. Without blinking an eye, my father, who was partial to the Crawford High School athletics and the football program because his son was playing on the team, directed that athletic director to my high school. The athletic director subsequently set up a dinner date with my parents.

At dinner he explained that not only would I have an opportunity to play football in my natural position as quarterback, but I also had a great opportunity to graduate with a degree of my choice. That impressed all of us. We sent films to the school, one thing led to another, and next thing we knew, a couple of us were on our way to Texas Southern University on full football scholarships.

CHAPTER II

MOTHER: BIRTH OF AN ENABLER

SON: LIFE ON LIFE'S TERMS

MOTHER: BIRTH OF AN ENABLER

My childhood was very different from that of my sons. My mother and father were divorced by the time I was three years old. My mother raised five of us with the help of my grandmother, grandfather, friends, neighbors, a wonderful short-lived stepfather (Daddy Richard) and several on-again, off-again boyfriends.

I was the third and final child my parents had, so for a while I was considered the baby in the family. My mother had two additional children after me and from time to time she had to resort to welfare to make ends meet. Receiving handouts always gave me a strong feeling of "less than." All of this mentally contributed to my childhood low self-esteem and identity problems. I did not have many material things so I suppose we were very poor. Yet through it all, I was raised with a good value system and was expected to be respectful, God fearing, and a high achiever.

In so many ways my childhood experiences, both positive and negative, shaped my parenting skills. Because I did not grow up in a stable environment, I internalized a lot of things and yearned for the days when I would be in control. I promised myself that when I grew up and had a family, my children would have stability, acceptance and success, period.

My parents' relationship could best be described as fast-paced, violent and dysfunctional. Yet in their special way both possessed a special gift for celebrating life, grabbing the gusto and having a ball. They knew how to throw a party and have a great time. I decided early on that I had better take life a little more seriously than my parents, so I concentrated on emphasizing trust, consistency, seriousness, independence, self control and the absolute fundamental need to be needed.

My father was an alcoholic who had suffered enormous psychological problems after a history of personal family tragedies. He was half black but passed for Italian, and after divorcing my mother, eventually married an Italian lady. I can recall how he referred to me as "his child by a colored woman." He used to fill my hopes with empty promises that always came crashing down.

Alcohol seemed to be the way he dealt with a lot of emotional problems from his past. As a teenager my father found his mother slain on the front porch and later learned that it had been at the hands of her lover. This occurred just a year after his own father had died. He did not have a steady home life and began to drink heavily.

I did not have any type of positive relationship with my father before or after my parents divorced. I would sit all day by the window on holidays, birthdays and Christmas waiting for a card, a gift or anything to come in the mail. He never sent a thing. He lived in Los Angeles, only a two-hour drive from my mother's San Diego apartment. I longed for the opportunity to stay extended times with him at his home in LA. The times I did spend with my father were few and far between and not very warm. Once I remember he would not let me ride with him on a bus because I was "too dark-skinned."

My mother, on the other hand, was a completely free spirit. She loved to have a lot of people surrounding her, and she raised us with the help of her mother, my loving Nana. We never really had a house to live in as we were growing up. We were apartment dwellers. My grandmother's house was what I considered my home and I loved spending my time there.

Even though I was one of the youngest children, I felt I could never be irresponsible. I felt like it was my job to make sure that everything was in place at all times. I had a need to live in an environment of perfection. Well, I thought I had experienced enough pain to last a lifetime and should not have to endure more. Besides, I felt that if you were real "good" and always looked the part, only "good" things could happen to you.

I met Rudy's father when I was 15 years old. We dated throughout high school and married when he and I graduated. It started as an ideal marriage, the Bill Cosby television Huxtable-type family, but it didn't end that way. It had all the right players, right? Split parental guidance, a protective mother, a father who tried desperately to be strict, a son Randy who was chronically ill and very emotionally needy, and Rudy the first born who was expected to excel at everything and did.

The brothers loved each other, but harbored resentment due to double standards and double messages, coupled with confused parents who stayed too long in an unhealthy relationship for all the wrong reasons. The boys' father and I were holding on to a dream and living an unhappy nightmare – staying together for the sake of the children and to maintain an acceptable family image in the community. We also stayed together because we were rather addicted to one another and because we did genuinely love each other in spirit. But it wasn't enough.

SON: LIFE ON LIFE'S TERMS

For most kids, heading off to college on a full scholarship would have been an opportunity for a fresh start. I thought I was one of them. I immediately got it in my mind that this would be an opportunity to clean up my act, play some football, get focused and obtain a degree.

But I was fully addicted to a mind-altering chemical, and I couldn't run from it. I soon learned I couldn't fly over three states and be protected from that "Jones."

Not long after our arrival on the campus of Texas Southern University in Houston, my close friend and I discovered the drug of our choice was not only available in and around the campus, but that we didn't have to look much further than the locker room. It was readily available because we weren't the only students indulging in our recreation of choice. Our habit from high school continued through freshman year.

I began to use marijuana on a much more frequent basis during summer football workouts before sophomore year. Many of my teammates also smoked weed. The houses that dealt marijuana were within walking distance from campus, literally minutes away. I will never forget going down to one of these houses and sliding my money under the door. Then

I'd watch for a small, manila package of marijuana we called a "nickel bag" to slide towards me from under the door.

After practice, we'd roll and smoke four or five joints from this nickel bag to "get our head on right," which translates into "shake off the day's activities." We had worked hard: During summer practice, in 105-degree heat and 85% humidity, we'd have three practice sessions a day with no breaks in between our classes. Then we'd get high in the evening, wake up the next morning, and do it all over again.

After a while, the high of marijuana grew old for me. I began to seek out my real drug of choice – rock cocaine. The taste and memory of the effects of that form of cocaine stayed with me. The Jones for this drug was always in the back of my mind. It jumped out like a large polar bear in the middle of Africa. With no tools of resistance in place, it began to rob me of my very being. It called me into action like a raging animal.

Before I knew it, I was scouring the streets of Houston looking for crack houses where I could buy rock cocaine or "crack." The majority of my sane or "down time" was spent thinking about the next opportunity to get high or blasted. I was caught in a cycle that was getting out of control.

There were clear signs of trouble: I became disinterested in my classes, and soon after, athletics. All my life I had been dedicated to sports. I should have known something was terribly wrong when I lost my passion for football.

Having older teammates who were already participating in mind-altering chemicals made it extremely easy for a new guy to come on board, take part in the drug festivities, and still perform on the field. However, having an addictive personality and being addicted started working against achieving my goals.

I want to make it perfectly clear that no one should blame Texas Southern University or the football team for my use of drugs. However, I do want to point out that no one is "protected" by going to a well-respected black university. Even the most sacred institutions in the United States have substance abuse problems. The question is, are they readily identifiable?

In my sophomore year at college, my routine was to stay out from 8:00pm to around 5:00am smoking crack. If I got an hour of sleep, I'd wake up and run with the team from 6:00am until about 7:00 or 7:30. After running, I hit the showers, followed by breakfast, then classes, then back to the training room at 2:00pm for taping and last minute instructions. At 3:00pm I would get on the field until 5:00. Again to the showers, then to dinner, followed by study hall from 7:00 to 8:00. About 8:00pm, I would go back out on the streets to begin the ritual all over again. That was my life for the better part of two and a half years in college.

I was very fortunate that neither my heart nor my brain exploded. Incredibly, I didn't even collapse on the field or on the street. I know now my Higher Power was looking out for me every step of the way, and for that I am truly grateful.

My life was pretty unmanageable with everything around me spinning out of control. I was not that same sharp, polished Rudolph Johnson III who had arrived on campus. I had become a closet monster – a crack monster. I had become someone who would go to almost any lengths to obtain my drug of choice.

I can still recall some of my out-of-control behavior patterns, which I am not proud of, during my drug using days. I would connive, steal, lie, cheat, anything it took to get my hands on material, merchandise or money that I could trade or barter for another blast. I even stole from people who were very close and who believed in me.

Often it involved conniving those who had complete trust in me, which turned me into someone that I could never be while in a sober frame of mind. That's when it slowly began to dawn on me that not only did I have a problem that was way out of control, but that I was also temporarily insane.

I'll share just a couple of the war stories with you so that you can gain some insight about being out of control because of substance abuse. I will protect the identity of individuals who were involved. I do not want to expose those people at the expense of my addictions, any further than has been necessary. I am out of the business of cheating people and destroying lives.

Painful as it is to recall, I consistently stole from my roommate in college. As the others who were close, he completely trusted me. He had lots of goodies that his parents sent him: VCR, TV, gold chains, watches, etc. Anything that wasn't nailed down in our room that was of value, I took and pawned. I collected so many pawn tickets that, to this day, I can't remember all the things that I left in various Houston area pawnshops. I could never keep it straight. I would always say to myself, I'll give the money back. But I didn't. I remember looking my roommate straight in the eye and telling him, "I don't know what happened to your gold chain" or your bracelet or TV. Eventually he suspected me but I would not admit the truth or that I had a problem.

I was so messed up that I'd con young, unsuspecting females who had crushes on me out of a ten or a twenty, then run directly to the drug man. I would trade romance for their financing my blasts. They believed in me and trusted me. They had no idea. These girls thought they really had a romance going on. I am sure they, too, put two and two together eventually and suspected something was seriously wrong. I want to say to all of the women that I misused in that manner, that I am so deeply sorry for taking advantage of them. This is my amends to them. Hopefully, one day they will read this book and understand that person wasn't the Rudy they thought they knew. It was a monster who was addicted to mind-altering chemicals.

My behavior and personality turned to being irritable and short-tempered. There were times when I would curse people for no reason. My mind was singularly focused on the next hit, the next high. I was not capable of thinking about business at hand.

To all those whom I have mistreated, I say from the bottom of my heart, I am very deeply sorry for putting you through that. I hope you understand that I was dealing with an illness. Again, to those individuals whom I misused and mistreated, I want to make an amends.

My family was not exempt from my bad behavior. I even stole from my mother on a Christmas visit home from college. I knew she had money in her purse for her shopping the next day. I crept into her room, went into her purse, took the money, went out, and got high all night long. The next day, I pretended I didn't know anything about it when the money came up missing. I even tried to make up a story of someone maybe sneaking into the house. My biggest, deepest apologies go to my mother.

CHAPTER III

MOTHER: FULL-BLOWN CODEPENDENCY

SON: FULL-BLOWN ADDICTION

Mother: Full-Blown Codependency

My codependent family fantasies continued during Rudy's first year in college. His grades were in good shape for a first-year student and he was always excited about returning home for special family affairs, major holidays, and part of summer vacation.

As a person who grew up without many things, I made a big deal of Christmas at our house. It was over the top and probably overcompensation. I insisted on having the largest tree available, and we had so many presents you could barely walk through the living room.

There was an incident that occurred during one Christmas holiday that should have left me with the feeling in the back of my mind that something was going on with Rudy, but I never allowed myself to think that he was having any problems he could not handle. It was Christmas Eve and I had been shopping all day. I returned home and fell fast asleep on the couch in the family room. I had $300 or $400 in cash in my purse, and when I woke up and went into my purse, the money was missing.

I asked everyone in the house if they had seen it, and they all assisted me in searching the entire house. I specifically remember Rudy saying, "Mom, maybe someone opened the patio door and took it." Never suspecting that Rudy, his friends or other family members had anything to do with it, I took it on myself saying, "I must have lost it while I was shopping."

The summer after Rudy's first year in college he appeared to be thinner than I remembered, but he was always a picky eater so I rationalized his change in appearance away very quickly. He worked the whole summer but he never seemed to have much money. He sort of isolated himself from the family and hung out with his friends. We just thought it was a young adult thing.

When he returned to school in the fall Rudy began to need a lot of cash assistance weekly, though it all seemed very legitimate to me. I thought boys will be boys, and after all, he was living on campus in another state.

Once I dared to ask myself, why does he need so much money? As quickly as the thought of anything negative emerged, I immediately went into my fantasy mode. I thought that if Rudy needed something that would enhance his college experience, I would not hesitate to help.

I remember one month when his Volkswagen broke down at least five times. Initially it seemed odd, but I quickly dismissed the thought and assured myself that what he really needed was a new car.

Rudolph Allister Johnson III probably had little chance of being anything other than an overachieving, people-pleasing, alcoholic addict, and I was obviously his enabler. In retrospect I must say that if you show me a full-blown alcoholic addict I will gladly identify a nearby full-blown codependent enabler.

While I hate to admit to it, there is something so satisfying in enabling. It gives one such pleasure. I would equate the satisfaction to that of the best deed you ever did. It's a great feeling you get when someone asks for your help and you assist him or her. Actually, not the feeling you get helping an ordinary person, but the especially warm feeling you get in your soul when you help a person who is disabled or incapable of helping himself or herself. It's almost like caring for a newborn infant. You know that the baby is totally dependent on someone else to fulfill its needs. The baby needs you to think for it, speak for it, teach it everything. You must feed it, provide love, clothing, diapering, everything, it's totally helpless. You can lose yourself in these feelings, and I did.

But to ensure a person's overall growth and successful development, adults or caretakers must move back and set boundaries. They must allow the baby to explore, and learn and make choices and become their own being. I tell you there is something fundamentally debilitating about being a full-blown codependent. In some ways my disease is far greater than Rudy's. But neither of us admitted our disease until things came to a crisis.

The ultimate codependent's secret is that we must be in control. Because of my need to control, I placed conscious and unconscious pressure on Rudy to succeed, and it caused him to internalize a lot of stress. A codependent's need for control is as necessary as air, water and food. We feel that by controlling everything and everyone around us we will be safe, unhurt, pain-free and, most importantly, not dependent. Independence is the wind beneath our wings. But to truly understand our disease you must understand what is on the other side of our need for control.

In our past we usually have been exposed to people, places or things that are out of control, inconsistent, and abusive. And we have the utmost fear of abandonment. So we raise at least one or two alcoholic/addicts because we need to be needed and we need to be codependent.

My son was, as I now think about it, my baby who needed me, all of us, and as painful as it may be to admit, we were not there for him. Oh, we thought we were, but in reality we were there for the parade and loved him, but with such conditions. I now wonder that maybe I thought Rudy III was so strong, I may not have told him enough that I loved him.

I think the safest way I had been able to show my love and support was to see that he had the best clothes and shoes, lots of toys, material things, and cash when he "needed" it.

My codependency "disease" was probably fostered by the fact that while I was growing up my family had very limited resources. I see that as an adult and a mother every time I bought a present for my children, I was buying a special present for the little girl living inside of me; the little girl who seemed to never have enough to eat or wear, enough personal attention, acceptance and most important, love. I guess it's safe to say that codependent parents are overindulgent. It doesn't matter how much money or resources there are, we still have an overindulgent predisposition.

I must confess that another secret that codependent, dysfunctional families share is that every family member has a role that is scripted to support the fantasies needed to maintain the secrets and denial. It does not matter what the family dynamics are; the outcome seems to be the same. The caretaker, be it both parents, one parent or another family member, is in full-blown dysfunctional and codependent denial, and the user is in full-blown addiction.

The disease of codependence is a burden – you carry your cross and you insist, against everyone else's will, that you carry their cross as well. I mean you literally will not bow out to others. You wrestle their responsibility away from them. You set very few boundaries and even when you do, you compromise them. You are inconsistent, too willing to enable and do your part and the other family member's part. Cleverly, that keeps everyone in his or her role of dependency, disease or disability.

I must confess that many times I was guilty of interfering when the boys' father attempted to teach them about manhood. I was probably thinking I was being fair, protecting them, and, to be really honest, not having a clue as to what I was really doing. So I must apologize to "big Rudy" and reveal that I did not know how to allow him to be the man of the house because of my lack of trust in men and my unresolved feelings of abandonment by my own father.

Now I know the importance of a father/son relationship and although he had his own character defects, I thank him for trying so hard. It must have been frustrating living with a strong-willed non-trusting co-dependent woman like me.

SON: FULL-BLOWN ADDICTION

I am thankful my Higher Power had something better in store for me after I completely bottomed out. I can say, firsthand, that substance abuse is a very serious, powerful, and cunning disease. It's not to be played with. It is not a laughing matter. It isn't something to be taken lightly. It is truly about life and death.

During spring training, right before my junior year, I had pretty much had enough. I was finally getting tired of the pattern, the addictive behavior, chasing the next blast. I had almost given up on my life. Then I received a phone call from one of our assistant coaches. He said, "Wait in your room, right where you are."

When the coach and another player arrived at my room, they got me off the bed and said seriously, "We noticed there's been a difference in your behavior, in your performance on the field. We noticed a difference in your studies as well. We don't know exactly what kind of problem it is, but we suspect that it's a drug problem."

At that moment, a great relief came over me. It was a feeling as if someone had lifted a tremendous weight off my shoulders. I thought, well, they finally figured this shit out. I finally got caught. Thank God someone was willing to assist me because I was about to give up on myself.

I was tired of the ripping and running. I was tired of the stealing, the conniving and the insane behavior. I was tired of the long sleepless nights; the crawling on the ground to find a piece of a rock that may have fallen from the dope tray. I was tired of yearning for that next hit. I was sick and tired of being in love with the drug. I was finally ready, once and for all, to surrender.

They took me over to the house of one of my fraternity brothers. Sitting me down, they explained, "Rudy, first thing in the morning you're going to call your parents to tell them what's been going on, and then we're going to get you some professional help."

The next morning when I woke up the sun seemed to shine brighter then I had ever seen it shine in Houston. I simply can't describe it. It was as if my Higher Power was saying, "I am going to bring you out of the darkness and into the fullness of light."

I picked up the phone and made the call to my parents. This was the most difficult call I ever made. I sat down and told them both the details of my problem and how seriously out of control I was. They were both extremely appalled. I could hear it in their voices. I am sure they were broken-hearted, but I never asked them about it. They were probably in disbelief and denial.

I explained that my coaches were taking me over to Houston International Hospital. I told my parents that I would call them once I got settled.

After hanging up the phone, I said to myself that it's time for Rudy to start taking care of Rudy. During the ride to the hospital, all kinds of things went through my mind, especially admitting I was truly an addict, and that I was ready to be cured. I was concerned with the kind of institution I would be staying in for the next thirty days. But my biggest question was, "Can I really beat this illness?"

As we pulled into the parking lot, my feet got colder. My will to recover turned into rage, disbelief and denial.

How did I let this happen to me?

CHAPTER IV

MOTHER: SILENT RESENTMENT AND ANGER

SON: FACING MY ADDICTION

MOTHER: SILENT RESENTMENT AND ANGER

Because of my self-imposed role as the family caretaker, I felt the stress and strain of being dependable, available and predictable. I longed for everyone around me to be weaned of my codependent "care-taking." I wanted to move swiftly through the letting-go process. Facing middle age, my desire for self-fulfillment, self-indulgence and freedom from responsibility was beginning to emerge.

My 40th birthday approached and I was so excited. We planned a huge birthday celebration. All of my family members and friends would be here, and I would get to be the star performer. I was going to dance a special birthday presentation. My family and friends are so understanding of my unfulfilled desire to be an African queen ballerina and international dancer/singer that they indulge me this pleasure from time to time. I'd been rehearsing for over two months. The music I selected was "Home" by Stephanie Mills.

It was rehearsing to "Home," and allowing God to lead my rhythms to express my feelings, that prepared me for a shocking telephone call from Rudy at college. It was about five a.m. California time when the phone started ringing. I was sleeping so well, you know, that deep, peaceful sleep.

I resisted waking up to answer the phone. In fact, I was so resistant that I put the ringing telephone into my dream, which appeased the persistent call for several rings. But the noise continued and my dream could no longer absorb the reality of the ringing telephone.

"Hello" I said, and instantly recognized my son's voice. Well, I thought, this would be a very special birthday, as my wonderful son is the first to call to wish me a happy birthday and to apologize for not being able to spend it with me and to tell me to have a great party.

But something was not right with his voice. Maternal instinct quickly kicked in and made me aware that my son was in trouble. I listened intently as he told me he had something important to tell me, that he *was* in trouble.

My heart began to sink, no, plunge. My imagination raced to every known definition of trouble housed in my brain. My thoughts raced ahead of his words, trying to know the details before he shared them, and at the same time rushing to form a solution to the unknown problem. The other part of me was cracking and falling apart, much like a ten-story apartment building crumbles when a demolition team sets off the dynamite.

Rudy told me that he was in his dormitory and that he was ordered by his coach to call home and tell his parents that he had a problem with drugs. The word "drugs" flashed on and off in my head like a neon sign. I froze in mid air, the world stood still, but Rudy kept talking. I didn't blink, I lost my voice and my feelings became numb.

Then I quickly switched into my enabler codependent mode and stepped out of, no abandoned, the role of mother. The mother role seemed far too helpless and vulnerable: Mother couldn't handle this situation.

My children's lives were supposed to be perfect, no harm could come to them, please! "Mother" would want to trade places with him. Give her life for his life. She would ask God to not let this happen. She would be angry with Him. She would not have a solid plan to rescue Rudy, unharmed, unblemished, untouched, no consequences.

So I selected the social worker-therapist part of me to come out because she was the best take-charge, corrective-action plan person. She also is a great codependent and enabler.

The social worker therapist began to ask all of the right fact-finding questions, slowly, carefully pushing the panicky mother's thoughts and feelings aside. The social worker began to devise a plan of action, able to take control of a crisis as it strikes.

Codependency was a safe place for me to hide all of my insecurities and real emotions and still function. However, I wanted to fall apart, die, take the addiction, jump in front of the danger, pack, run, and move to a place in the universe where no one knew me. Move to a place where I could not be reached by telephone or by letter, unable to receive good or bad news.

I wanted to go limp like a rag doll, have a breakdown, take to my bed, be hospitalized, fed intravenously, rolled around in a wheelchair. But I did not, could not.

I also wanted to seek out drug dealers, the number one enemy. I wanted to hurt someone. I had nightmares in which I took automatic machine guns and annihilated the enemy drug dealers. I sought them out, captured them one by one in my dreams.

I felt so much anger. Normally a compassionate non-violent person, I had to control every thought and action. My mind, body, soul and spirit were on full alert. It was a true case of fight or flight. I continued to have dreams holding a machine gun, rounding up drug dealers, backs against the wall and annihilating them. They would wake me up in a cold sweat, shaken, distraught. To even consider such violent thoughts was alarming to my soul. This anger was bigger than I was. It consumed me.

My world was upside down. I was stuck in a black hole. Anger distorted my perception of reality and I was afraid it would ultimately destroy me. I knew that I had to begin to seek a positive way to dismantle this anger. I had to take the first step toward healing. I had to admit that I was powerless with what happened to Rudy's life, that only God could intervene, and that in order for him to intervene, I had to get out of the way.

Even though I believe in God, trust him, have faith in His ability to heal and take care of all my needs, as a mother I did not think anyone could take better care of my child than I could. I had this feeling that only I as a mother could assist my child to safety. I understood the relationship with God, but I still had this desire to hold on to the outcome. I would give Rudy to God and then take him back.

I began to search a little deeper into my angry feelings to sort through the wreckage. It was painful to search because of the truths I discovered.

I was angry with myself for exposing Rudy as a child to the people, including family members, who were casual drug users during the intellectual enlightened sixties. I began to blame his experimentation and subsequent addiction on me. If only I had been more careful of his environment and social interactions. Maybe I could or should have stayed home and not pursued my educational career goals. Did I take him to church enough? Had I made God angry? Was God punishing me for some past wrong? The devil was attacking my mind.

I had to admit I was powerless to all outcomes in my family life, and the lives of others. My "babies" I had to let go and let God. I had to face my disease of codependent "rescuing." I had to test my faith in God; I had to work through my anger. I had to do all of it if Rudy was to have any chance at full recovery.

I also had to look further at my anger, and what I found really unraveled me, I was also angry with Rudy. That was one of the hardest things I had to face in my life. It was okay to be angry at myself, it was okay to be angry at family and friends, it was okay to be angry at God, but to be angry at my baby, my child, this young adult who was attached to my soul, connected to my spirit, had been carried in my womb, breathed with me, shared my vascular system and every heartbeat. I had to face the fact that he had disappointed me and that I was in fact angry with him for becoming a drug addict.

It was not in the script. He was supposed to soar like an eagle, become a part of the protected ones, and be perfect. In retrospect, I knew it was this kind of thinking, these unrealistic expectations, that could cause a child to seek drug experimentation.

I did have good intentions. I wanted the best for Rudy, with minimal obstacles and emotional pain, forgetting that children must get out in the world and experience life's challenges in order to develop positive character, spiritual awareness and inner strength. But the reality is, they can get lost.

Emotional pain led me to explore past resentment and anger I had stored up, stacked away, as a child and young adult. It's amazing how much stuff we shove into our personal closets. We pack our experiences neatly and carefully away, hoping, praying, never to revisit them again. Yet we always do.

I had stuffed and stacked so many resentments and disappointments into my closet that nothing else could fit. The door literally would not close. I hid the door with the greatest camouflage of all, strength. When my friends, family, neighbors and community members looked at me, they saw this woman, mother and friend who had it all together. I knew all the right words to say, all the right expressions to show, and the correct nonverbal gestures.

With Rudy's admission of his disease, I could finally break the hidden closet door off its hinges, and pull out painful things that clung to the shelves of my inner mind. Not caring what anyone else thought, I had to free myself of "What will my friends say?" "Am I a failure as a mother and a parent?" "Will this destroy Rudy's opportunity to heal and find his way to success again?"

I was breaking out from what I did not fully understand. I knew that I had finally reached my level of codependent saturation. I was drowning in my own strength, suffocating in my let's-do-it-all, know-it-all self.

But I didn't know this possible new person, this free me, this person who was not holding the lid on the pressure cooker, who does not need to appear in control, who does not need to fix everything or prevent uncomfortable or bad things from happening to people she cared about. I was afraid of this new person at first, yet too exhausted, in too much pain, to hold her back. She must be given permission to come out, to be human, to experience all of life's joy and pain. To not be a therapist – just a woman, a mother, friend, neighbor, lover, daughter, sister, an aunt.

What a revelation. I didn't have to hold on to a marriage of 25 years just so the children could grow up whole in a perfect family with mommy and daddy. Quite the contrary, this dysfunctional family actually made everyone in it miserable, depressed and diseased.

After Rudy's telephone call and admission of drug usage, I immediately contacted my insurance company and told them that my son needed to be hospitalized due to depression and drugs. I had them hold a hospital bed and then organized his dad and younger brother Randy to fly to Texas to be with him through the initial hospitalization treatment. I wanted to go, but then a codependent does what is best for others. I thought that my husband needed to go with our younger son, and the three guys could be together, help each other, and work through everything. Then everything would be perfect. True co-dependents believe in Fantasy Island and happy endings.

When my husband and Randy returned, they reassured me that Rudy III would be all right. Rudy had a great recovery support team in Texas: his terrific coach, the athletic director, and his fraternity brothers. And he had met a wonderful best friend, confidante, and lover, Sheryl Mallory.

As Rudy worked his program and began the long road to recovery, something phenomenal began to happen. Rudy's disease and my co-dependency had held our dysfunctional family together. Our recovery, our healing would dismantle it. The Johnson's – the devoted wife, the doting mother, the dedicated husband/father, the loving intelligent and perfect child, the house on the hill, two cars, the pool and the nice neighborhood. All of these things would be examined with different eyes. Each one of us would face our own issues.

We all could finally crack up and begin the healing process.

Yes, this wonderful Donna Reed, Father Knows Best and Cosby-inspired fantasy family that I dreamed of having as a child, worked so hard to build, put all of my personal dreams on hold for, sacrificed my career for, would probably not stand up to close scrutiny. It could not, would not, survive the truth. It would be my personal Watergate, Bay of Pigs – a dismantled dynasty.

As I began my healing journey I had to face my relationship with my husband. We really didn't have a relationship. We were dedicated to the idea of family, but we lived very separate lives. We had fallen out of love years before this tragedy. This marriage was now based on a lie. It would have to end.

I decided to seek individual therapy. It was one of the best gifts I ever gave myself. Dr. Diane Evans guided me through all of my childhood nooks and crannies and led me to invitations of healing. I was starved for emotional healing, self-love, reality, truth, and the freedom to express honestly.

The funny thing about my deciding to enter therapy was that at first I tried to get everyone in the family to participate. I tried to get my middle son Randy to go and I begged my husband to go. Finally my therapist said, "Maybe you should come by yourself." When she said those words I felt fear and relief. It had to be done. I knew I was on my way to the healing zone. I could see the light at the end of the tunnel. I could actually see myself in spirit, healthy and whole.

My therapist guided me into people, places and things that I had long forgotten. She carefully led me into every dark corridor, reality blazing, blaring truth and blinding emotional trauma. We visited places, sad places, happy places, until I could no longer hold onto half-truths, lies and make-believe. Rudy's addiction, my codependency and our individual desire to heal, would cause this family pause, catch all the members off guard and throw each one of us for an emotional loop.

I had to face, embrace, forgive and let go of most of my childhood resentments and anger. I came to a new understanding that I was personally powerless to determine the fate and future of others.

In order to heal, I had to embrace God's love, truth and positive energy. If we do this, we not only survive, we can live life to the fullest, fly with our dreams and soar to our real purpose in life.

I admitted I was angry with myself, and once I faced that truth, I worked through the pain. I did not need to, nor was I able to, save the world. I was free from lies, half-truths, and most importantly, secrets. My denial, codependency, and secrets had contributed to Rudy's addiction. As a mother I had given him life. Now, with truth revealed, I could help him find his soul.

We would have to fall apart to heal. Crack-up. Rudy would no longer be required to snag the starring role. His brother could no longer stand in his shadow, act helpless, and seek negative attention. I could no longer be the enabler.

Each of us would have to find our truths and begin to put the pieces of our lives back together again.

SON: FACING MY ADDICTION

My coaches escorted me to Houston International Hospital to begin the recovery process. I knew nothing about recovery or the Twelve-Step Program. This whole process was new to me. It's funny how that institution still stands out in my mind. I became very reluctant about being checked into a facility.

I knew I had some problems but at first I questioned that I was an addict or alcoholic, therefore, I didn't understand what the fuss was all about. I was doing well academically and athletically, so I thought. One minute I was walking on campus, on top of the world, on the football team, just pledged a fraternity. The next minute, BOOM!! I needed help. I was being taken to an institution for a very serious illness that had almost destroyed my life. Here I was, nineteen years of age, being admitted to a recovery program in a hospital with no family around.

Suddenly, out of the blue, I was hearing that not only was I an alcoholic and drug-abuser, but also a failure in society. This was my interpretation of the situation in my mind. To me alcoholics and addicts were the winos on the corner who didn't have a dime in their pocket and begged every person passing by for money just so they could buy a shot. They were homeless, pushing around shopping carts. They were dirty and not groomed. They smelled bad. That wasn't me.

I was admitted to the hospital in the evening, and it had gotten dark. The coach had filled out and signed the paperwork. He gave me a hug, shook my hand and said, "Rudy, I have to go but I promise to come back tomorrow." I appreciated hearing that, even though I was in a fog. This coach proved to be very dedicated and very committed to my well-being and to my recovery.

That first night I spent in the institution there were so many conflicting thoughts racing through my head. My first thought was that of denial. I felt I didn't need to be there. "As soon as I get a chance, I'm going to leave this place," I said to no one in particular.

In San Diego, my family was packing and purchasing their plane tickets. They were coming to make sure that everything was all right. I looked around my hospital room and guessed everything was not all right.

In fact, I said to myself that something along the way went entirely wrong.

I can remember not talking to my hospital roommate – I didn't even acknowledge that I had a roommate until day three. Actually, I didn't acknowledge anyone around me at all.

I had to start to get into myself from a different perspective. I couldn't help wondering what was being said about me on campus; he's a drug addict, he's an alcoholic, he's this, he's that. Much to my surprise, I found out later that everyone was relieved I was getting help.

My fraternity line brother and my coach came the next day. I was flooded with calls from well-wishers, friends and family members. Thinking about how loved I was, and still am, gets me very emotional to this day.

I finally relaxed a bit after the first weekend. I made up my mind that I did need help. I did need to attack this from a strategic perspective and to work the program. Though I didn't know much about working the program, I resolved to do whatever I needed to do to assure that within thirty days I would be ready to leave.

Reality set in and I admitted that I was a sick individual. This was the hardest thing to admit. The tears welled up, but you know us black men, we don't just stand up and cry. We don't want to reveal too much. We cry in our sleep or we'll sneak around and shed a few tears, but it's no wailing like a baby.

You know, sometimes I say to myself, we black men have it hard – we cannot just let go even in the most severe circumstances, like this. We have to show that we're always in control of a situation.

Determined, I shut myself away from the outside world for thirty days. It was like being in jail. When I listen to people talking about jail or an institution, I can relate. I was locked up, no rights, no freedom. I did not leave that hospital. I was allowed to play a little basketball, to take walks in a controlled environment, but never on my own.

I had to face that I had lied, cheated and stole from people who mattered in my life. I was ashamed because I hadn't been able to hold anything in my hands longer that two seconds without it being pawn material. Eventually I couldn't hold on to a dime, or bother to keep myself well groomed, or in clean clothes or get a haircut.

I was mortified at what I had become. I was never raised to be a liar, a thief or a cheater. I was humiliated with myself for taking things that did not belong to me. That was the behavior of the addict that I had become. It was definitely time to face myself with this illness of drug and alcohol addiction, and its consequences. It was time to face Rudy. Unto this day I am ashamed, and that's why it's tough to walk through this process.

When people talk about recovery in Alcoholics Anonymous (AA), getting to the fourth step in the Twelve-Step Program is the hardest. The fourth step entails revealing and dealing with the humiliation, the pain, and all the crap that keeps the vicious cycle turning. Often when I felt strong enough to start looking at it, I would stop because it was too deep to handle. In a way, this book is my "complete" fourth step.

I had to become real with the shame. The reality is, I have an illness that drastically affected my personality. The person I have become today, who keeps himself clean and well groomed is the one who has money in his pocket and can give it to someone on the street who is in need. I can now share with individuals who are less fortunate then I am. I try to keep my family straight. I try not to lie to others. I try not to get in any position that would allow me to cheat another individual out of their money. All that is the result of the shame, anger and hatred during my using days.

After thirty days being institutionalized, I was released to go back out into the world to attempt to stay sober on my own. Quickly I realized that I didn't do something right. I simply wasn't ready. I came to the realization that I was doing this for everyone but me. I didn't *really* hit bottom. It was a soft fall. So when I was released from the treatment center, I said to myself, now I can leave with this illness in control.

It was my "stinking" thinking, as they call it in the program. My rationale was, I can drink but I can't do that crack. Then once I started drinking, I rationalized that I could have a smoke of marijuana, but just couldn't do crack.

A month after I was released from the hospital I took a flight home. One thing about the program that you soon learn is that you can't go back to the old people, places and things early in your recovery process. But there I was, heading back to the epicenter of my addiction, San Diego, where I had learned how to use drugs.

And I had a lot hanging over my head.

My college classes were incomplete because I had to leave school to recover. My football scholarship was in question – the school didn't know whether they could take a chance on an alcohol and drug addict. They didn't know if they wanted me back, even after all the help they had given me. I had become a liability. I can understand what the coach must have been feeling. If I put myself in his position, I don't think I'd want an addict or alcoholic on my team.

I hadn't seen my family since all this happened. I had been locked up in Houston, communicating via telephone. I didn't really get a chance to talk about the whole situation.

Arriving in San Diego, my "stinking" thinking awakened, telling me it was okay to be with my old friends and partners. Though they were drinking their beers and smoking their joints, my stinking thinking was telling me that I could hang around if I didn't have any.

Yes, one thing led to another and before I knew it, I was back out in the streets. In the program, it's called relapse. I had come back to the environment of the same people, places and things that had exposed me to the addiction initially, and had a relapse because I wasn't serious about the program. And my old California buddies didn't respect my program. As a result, I found myself getting into trouble again.

We began forging checks and using the money to buy drugs. In San Diego there was a guy I knew who could get access to checks in bulk. We forged them, went to a check-cashing place, and cashed them for ready drug money. Near the end of the summer we were arrested by the San Diego Police and taken to county jail.

Eventually I was released on my own recognizance. My grandmother and parents put up the bail money and a trial date was set for me. Once again, here's my "Higher Power" stepping in to make an attempt to save me. Once again, my coach of Texas Southern came through for me. He wrote a letter explaining my past admission to the recovery program at the hospital in Houston. He accounted for me being a football player and being enrolled in school. Quite unexpectedly he took full responsibility for my well-being upon my release from the court on probation. Subsequently, the courts dropped the charges from a felony to a misdemeanor. I was released under the responsibility of the coach, on a one-year probation and permitted to travel outside California.

I went back to Houston where, by the grace of God, the university decided to give me another chance. My behavior was highly monitored. I did well that semester. But when winter break came around, that same stinking thinking entered my mind again, only one year after my dramatic episode of being locked up.

Instead of coming back to San Diego, I decided to stay in Houston. Every time I would stay in Houston, it was in one of two places, either with my coach or with my distant cousin. This time, even though my coach was my legal guardian, we decided that I would go live with my cousins because it was going to be a long break. He wanted me to be as close to my family as possible.

But I was manipulating everyone. I persuaded them that it would be better if I stayed with a relative. In the back of my mind I was thinking, how can I put myself in the best position to go back out and use?

Well, everyone at my cousin's had been alerted to my illness. I had been drinking beer during the season, and everybody knew it. They would say, "Have a brew, but just don't mess with that cocaine." That was the insane part about it. After coming in from a game, they'd say, "Yo, Rudy, here's a brew!" They didn't understand about addiction at that time and I don't blame them. Even my coach knew that I was drinking beer and he was OK with it. They would rather see me drink alcohol then be on rock cocaine. They didn't understand that even a beer would set me up for a relapse. Eventually, I would find my way back to the drug of choice.

Two of my teammates and I had this grand scheme about my applying for a student loan. It worked, I had two thousand dollars coming down the pike. I was staying with family who really didn't understand my disease. I had set myself up to be away from my coach. This all allowed me to play a little.

Then I was notified that the student loan check had arrived. At first, I panicked. I honestly tried to do right. I actually considered telling the coach that my check was in. I even thought we'd go get the check together. That he could deposit it into his account and provide me with an allowance, as I needed it.

Unfortunately, this didn't happen. I picked up my check, went to the bank, cashed it and put two thousand dollars cash directly into my front pocket. Then I drove around the city drinking beer.

It was simply a matter of time. The more I drove, the more I drank. I believe I drank three or four beers while hanging out with partners and friends. Next thing you know, I got a hold of some cocaine and ended up on a three-day binge. I spent every bit of that two thousand dollars.

When I finally came out of the drug haze, it was after the holidays, January 12, 1987. I never will forget that day. I remember looking at myself in the mirror and saying, who are you? What have you done with all the chances your Higher Power has given you?

I had just blown two thousand dollars and could not remember most of it. All I could remember was that it was one big party after another. I had been running around trying to see the "dope man" with money in my pocket. When you go to those crack houses with money, anything can happen. With two thousand dollars in my front pocket, it started out one little blast, then another and another. Of course, I told myself I was going to stop which, obviously, I never did. I wasn't even eating. Naturally, I had lost weight.

Once again, I wasn't taking care of myself and my family was worried because I hadn't been home in a number of days. They didn't know what was going on. Looking at myself in the mirror, I told myself I was going to go to an AA meeting. Luckily, a year later, I still had the option of returning to the program. I knew what I had to do. I knew whom I had to do it for…myself, with the guidance of my Higher Power.

By this time, going to a meeting was not a struggle. I had not the strength left in my body to fight it. I was through fighting. I surrendered to my Higher Power. I don't know what made me tell myself to go to a meeting. Some people say that I had finally hit my rock bottom.

I went to the Post Oak Club, where AA meetings were held in Houston, Texas. A lot of white people attended. They accepted this young black man from California. I would sit in the back of the room, but wouldn't say anything. I would just sit there. All the times before I would come in trying to talk to, and manipulate, people. But now I began to listen to some of these white guys explain their lives. I remember them saying how they had achieved ten, fifteen, twenty years of sobriety. I wondered if they were telling the truth. I thought to myself, my goodness, somebody is lying in here – they just know how to manage their high.

But I can now say I know firsthand that black men can get sixteen years of sobriety too, because I have. Black men can recover from what I consider to be one of the most powerful addictions out there. The irony is that I thought heroin was the epitome of addiction. One day at a time, by the grace of God, I was able to stay away from the most powerful, most dangerous, and the most harmful man-made drug, rock cocaine. Though I am still subject to fall, I will let my Higher Power work with and through me.

Today I tell those I sponsor to write down ten things that you don't want to do, but that you need to do the most. How many sober people actually do this? Not a sick person, but a sober person. We are scared to answer those questions. We don't really want to know what's inside ourselves.

I had to go make amends to the people that I knew I hurt as a result of my addiction. Unto this day, I'm still doing it. For their healing and mine, I want to tell all those I misused during my addiction days, "I'm sincerely sorry for mistreating and hurting you."

For the most part, when we look at one another, we judge each other based on our work and our actions. And making amends is taking action. That's what is important to me now.

Facing my addiction was not easy back then. But I was lucky I was not alone – my teammates and coaches never left my side. One fraternity line brother held my hand and stayed with me through all the ups and downs. These guys were like family, supporting me through my roughest times.

CHAPTER V

MOTHER: FACING MY CODEPENDENCY

SON: FAMILY RELATIONSHIPS

MOTHER: FACING MY CODEPENDENCY

Being a codependent parent is so intense, so paralyzing, that you eventually become immobilized. You have tried every known solution to man – black magic, personal sacrifice, pleading, dealing, worrying, preaching, begging, crying, hoping, and wishing, until you finally come to grips with two things: you are powerless to outcomes in your life and you are powerless to the outcome of your children's lives. You must submit and let go.

Now, there is a big difference between that and giving up on your addicted son or daughter. As parents, we must never give up on our children. However, turning them over to your Higher Power, whom I call God, is very different. It means that you stop enabling and rescuing.

So for me, facing my codependency, revealing my family secrets and lies, facing the truth about Rudy's disease, my disease and our family dysfunction, forced me into healing myself. I offered Rudy assistance in working a program of sobriety, without trying to work that program for him.

I suppose I should explain in detail what I mean by letting go and letting God. It sounds rather mystical and esoteric, but it's simple. It is a process.

This family, my family, had long ago cracked up. I felt I was literally holding it together. Each time an emotional seam burst, I patched and pretended that all was well. The insanity of it all is that all the family members, Rudy, my middle son Randy, the "baby" Rashad, and my husband Rudy Jr., were all looking at me through the cracks, each in their own personal emotional pain, begging me to acknowledge the end. That it's over, it's broken; to let all the pieces go. They were begging to be allowed to face reality, show their character defects and their trauma, uncover their pain and secrets.

But I held on a little longer, I pleaded with them to remain in their "perfect" roles, I begged for more time, assuring them with unspoken words that I could endure and make it all better.

Finally, after completing my last counseling session and my reality check with my Higher Power, I knew it was time. A time for cracking up. A time to heal. I remember that day very well. It was a warm sunny day in Southern California, not too hot, a nice ocean breeze.

My husband and I had long since stopped sharing the same bed, but I insisted that we share the same house to look the perfect couple/family. Rudy was away at college battling his disease and being a successful student. My middle son, Randy, was away at a college he hated but agreed to attend because of my fantasy-planning insistence. He was experimenting with drugs and drowning in pain. Baby Rashad was still living a sheltered life as a five year old.

That morning felt like every other codependent day in my life. I would wake up, plan my strategy for coping with life one day at a time, map out the other family members' lives and in general attempt to take control of all activities. I even attempted to foresee negative energy or events headed toward me, and my children.

When I stretched and walked down the hallway, something inside felt different. I looked around the house, my dream house, the perfect backdrop for the perfect family and I felt detached, like I didn't belong. I have no idea where that feeling came from; but suddenly I knew what I had to do. If I was going to survive, live, be whole, if my children were to heal, I must leave today.

I had been swimming too many laps in the pool of life and I was tired, in the deep end, in a panic, drowning. My basket was filled to capacity. I no longer had the desire, will, need or strength to hold this dysfunctional family together.

With newfound conviction I packed some of my things, baby Rashad's clothes and toys, books and a portable TV and loaded the car in broad daylight.

After years of wondering what my family, friends and neighbors would think if my husband and I separated or divorced, here I was filling the car to the brim, waving goodbye to my curious neighbors. Some had shock on their faces, disbelief, confusion and a look of "what's happening to that perfect couple, the perfect family?" Yet none had the nerve to come out and ask. If they had, they would have met with my new attitude of not really caring what anyone else thought. I knew that what I was doing was right, necessary and healing.

Baby Rashad and I moved in with my mother and grandmother. We moved out of my dream house on the hill into the small two-bedroom one-bath house I had called home as a small child. Extended family in familiar surroundings was comforting. It was in this house, with my mother and grandmother as my support system, that I was able to face my failed dysfunctional marriage.

I then began to pursue new personal goals I didn't know existed. My husband and I divorced. Over the next year I worked with two excellent therapists, Dr. Dianne Evans and Dr. Norman Chambers, and with God, to pick up the shattered pieces of my life and restore my sanity. Eventually I saved enough money to buy my ex-husband out of my dream home and move back into it with Rashad, where I still live today.

But that first night out of my house, I literally lay flat on my stomach, not on my knees, and surrendered to God. I vowed this time to not take it back.

I could not fix another thing. I didn't have another answer, I could not think of another plan. I let God take over my body, mind and spirit, and while I was flat on the floor, surrendering, my son Rudy was beginning his walk into the healing light.

Rudy had found a wonderful healthy non-codependent girlfriend who stood by his side during his whole ordeal. He also had the unconditional love and support of the Texas Southern University coaching staff, his fraternity brothers and a great sponsor.

His coach was there for Rudy from the beginning to the end. To me, the exhausted, surrendered, codependent mother, Rudy's coach was God-sent, a guardian angel. He helped my son, and to me he is a hero. He busted Rudy using, confronted him, offered help, supported him through detoxification and a 30-day hospitalization, coordinated his academic affairs and stayed in constant contact with me to assure me all was well.

In retrospect, I don't know if I was there for Rudy as much as a mother as I was as a therapist. I think he has a silent resentment that I expected too much from him and gave him too little motherly nurturing. For this and much more, I need to make some of my own amends.

First, to "Big Rudy," as I affectionately call Rudy's father. In my sick codependent state I never allowed you to assume your full role as my co-partner and co-parent. For this I emotionally failed you and caused you great pause in your overall development into manhood.

I now understand why you turned to other women, who empowered you. As I never had a father/daughter nurturing relationship, I had an unrealistic expectation of your role as a father. In addition, I should have set clearer boundaries after the first affair you had. I should have insisted upon counseling or a divorce. No, I stayed and made you pay with your manhood for your infidelities.

I wanted to keep my fantasy family and make you pay on a daily basis for the affairs. Instead of forgiving and starting over, I made you remember and "pay" each day.

Rudy III, in my mission to make you into the perfect child, I don't think I nurtured you enough. It was difficult for me to be intimate with you and easier for me to be your therapist, your guide.

Randy, I was overprotective of you. I made you lose your self-confidence and responsibility. I made you feel incapable.

Rashad, I hope that I am more balanced with you, as you came along during our healing period. However, the jury is still out on how well I have served you in my role as your mother/friend.

Rudy's admittance and disclosure of his secret addiction released me; it set me free. It may sound strange, but I was the kind of person who stayed in a bad relationship for the kids' sake, although I counsel other people to never stay for the kids. I did not follow my own advice.

Rudy's trouble made me face the fact that our family was dysfunctional, the children were not okay. Having a mother and father does not guarantee that your children will grow up emotionally stable, healthy and successful. Quite the contrary, if you stay for the sake of the children and you are in a dysfunctional family, chances are that your family will eventually harbor resentments, emotional trauma and repressed pain.

I began the process of setting boundaries for the people I loved. I needed to allow my family members to accept their own consequences. No longer could I hold a safety net under each family member in anticipation of potential danger or to catch each fall. They could finally experience life on their own, embracing fully their own rewards and consequences.

I am often asked by people, "How do you deal with a family member who is addicted? What can you do? How do you help him or her without rescuing or giving up your own life? How do you maintain your own life and not get caught up into the addictive behavior?"

I can relate to all these questions. We co-dependents almost forget to breathe when someone we love is in crisis. For me, I had to take the first step and realize that I was *a separate person.*

That may sound weird, but a good codependent feels like there is a spiritual umbilical connection to their addicted family member. If they are in pain, so are we. If their life is in chaos, so is ours; if they are in crisis, so are we; If they are homeless, we should not be allowed to sleep in a comfortable bed; if they are hungry, we should not enjoy our meals. If they are out on a binge, we should deny ourselves sleep, food and enjoyable moments of each day.

We feel we should fall apart, remain in pain, be sad, mourn and wait to help. What a helpless state of being. How self defeating and unproductive. Just think, we become more like the person who is sick, diseased and out of control. And, as Rudy taught me, when we are in our codependent state of mind, we enable the user to continue to use people, places and things.

Rudy taught me that if I really wanted to help him, I had to help myself first. Look in my own backyard; deal with my own addiction of codependency. He told me that if I helped myself, continued to love him, set clear boundaries, worked my own program of recovery, addressed my own issues of enabling, then it would give him less guilt, less resentments and assist him in his quest to reach the healing zone.

A child shall lead the way.

Initially, I would get mad as hell at him. Who did he think he was? How arrogant! What a smart ass! He was the one with the problem and yet he was dictating to me, writing my script, taking control. Was I out of control?

Yes, I was out of control, yet using control as a way to cope, a way to hide my pain. Getting beyond my anger, I was able to hear Rudy. I followed his advice and it worked.

So, when anyone asks, "What can I do?" I say, "Ask not what you can do for your diseased loved one: Ask what you can do for your diseased codependent self, and then you can help both yourself and your loved one."

I am not suggesting that families treat their loved ones mean. Just be realistic, truthful and honest! Let them know that they are sick (addicted), that you are sick (codependent), that you love them, and that you will support them when they can admit they are addicted and want or seek treatment. That you will set boundaries with them while they are using and abusing, and that you will seek help for them, i.e., attend community self help groups, church groups, pray for them, learn more about their disease, etc.

Let them know that you are available to go to meetings with them. Find out about local recovery programs. Keep a list of recovery contacts, telephone numbers and addresses of people and places that are available to help them. Buy them recovery books and information. Be loving, firm and consistent and finally let go and let God! Remember, as Rudy helps me to understand, you are powerless to all outcomes.

Finally, we must learn to relax, let go, breathe, stay in the moment and try to enjoy the wonders, lessons and joys that each day brings. Admit we can't cure the addict, rescue the addict, prevent the addict from relapsing and most importantly, we must realize we are not the addict! Thanks again Rudy, for helping me heal and understand your disease, my disease, and for setting me free.

Son: Family Relationships

The relationship with my family is a subject that I haven't spoken much about up to this point. Well, the discussion is strictly one-sided, from my perspective. My family has been there for me every step of the way, from addiction to recovery and from recovery to addiction, back to recovery again.

I want to touch upon my relationship with various family members including my mom and dad, my wife Sheryl, my son, Little Rudy and daughter, Mallory, my middle brother, Randy, and my youngest brother, Rashad.

To help describe my frame of mind and where I'm coming from, I want to mention some personal circumstances that I dealt with prior to my recovery period. One of these circumstances is that I was the first grandchild to receive a college degree. One might say, "Well, that's not such a tremendous task." However, I'm not the oldest grandchild on either side of my family. In fact, I'm right in the middle on both sides. I witnessed family members before and after me attempt a college education. I am the first of two to complete college thus far. The significance of this is that I feel I was not acknowledged much for the accomplishment of graduating from a university, yet everyone was quick to acknowledge my addiction.

I vividly recall my grandmother, my father's mother who has since passed away, sharing graduation with me. Grandma Ruth was a very special person in my life. I wanted to demonstrate to her that I was doing all that I could to recover and stay out of the entrapment of a drug-addicted life. I wanted to keep her loving arms around me through my adulthood. In my mind, those arms are still around me.

The rest of the family, I believe, was proud of the fact that I was going to school and playing ball, but I don't think they ever really understood how significant this was to me. From my perspective, I believe it caused me to feel great resentment. I won't say they didn't play a key role, because they did. The encouragement and support didn't seem to exist throughout the family. I don't blame them. I'm simply stating that acknowledgment was important to me.

Rudolph A. Johnson Jr., my dad, I love very much. He is the kind of father I think every child wanted to have while growing up. He was way ahead of his time in terms of fatherhood. In the late sixties and early seventies, African-American males typically ran from their parental responsibilities. My dad decided to stay and be there as a father. He was there for my middle brother and I from small babies, changing our diapers, all the way to manhood, through thick and thin. Naturally, we had our share of conflicts as in all family relationships, but he was there for us.

For the record, there were some negative things too. I'd say that his continued use of certain mind-altering chemicals definitely had an influence on me. I won't go so far as to say that I imitated him and as a result of that imitation became addicted. Rather, I'd say that seeing this activity as acceptable in our household definitely put me in a relaxed position about the subject.

My dad liked to keep things inside. He had a way of not showing a lot of emotion when we were growing up. He didn't cry in front of us. He didn't really let himself go. Again, this is the pride of the black man not showing tears or emotion. He was always a strict disciplinarian in a structured environment. In fact I remember asking myself, is he like this around everyone?

It was tough being his kid. To be named Rudy III after him was extra pressure. I wanted to achieve a lot of the things I had seen him achieve in his lifetime. I truly looked up to him. But it was very much a negative not to see his emotions.

It was during my high school years that I could see the love was crumbling in my parents' marriage. It was as plain as the nose on my face that they did not have much time left together. The marriage was literally dissolving. Little things would send them into major arguments. They just weren't happy anymore. It was like two individuals living together just because they felt they had to be together.

They were not together because they loved each other or enjoyed each other's company any longer. At the same time, they had become attached at a very young age. They knew nothing else except each other. In retrospect, in my adulthood, seeing them interact, I'd say that they are still in love and neither one of them wants to be the first to admit it.

There are definitely some family highlights. My dad stood by us as a family instead of running, when things weren't going great. For that, I admire and respect him. And my father went to college, completed his undergraduate work, and finished his masters in social work. He hit the ground running before tearing right through the professional scene as the Vice President of Neighborhood House Association. He later became the CEO/President of the San Diego Urban League before he decided on a career with the City of San Diego as the Youth Programmer. I greatly respect his career.

My father had a way of making you feel like there was this protective arm around you at all times. While he carried a lot of things inside, holding things in, he really worked to make things right for everyone else. He would sacrifice himself. This type of behavior had its good and bad effects, such as taking a toll on his health. He is the kind of man who, when he has a dollar in his pocket, everyone has a dollar in their pocket. When money is available he likes to have a good time until it slowly runs out. It was always good to be around my dad when he was in a good, happy mood with money in his pocket, feeling sociable.

Anything that I am or that I've done related to sports is definitely my father's victory. He nurtured me, coached me, and guided me through the maze of the sports scene. His encouragement led me to a college scholarship, which subsequently led me to a civil engineering degree, and the ability to provide for my own family.

My mom, Lorraine R. Johnson, with whom I'm writing this book, I love with all my heart. It has been a challenge for the two of us to sit down and discuss this project. We had a lot of emotions to work through, but we did it successfully.

I love the lady tremendously. I simply wish she would slow down sometimes and take a breath. My mom was the type of mother who always provided counseling. She's a therapist by training, but even by nature she was a counselor. She always gave guidance. She would gather together an entire neighborhood to discuss some of the negative things that were going on in the area and hold court, right there in her own living room. Everyone loved that. They were fascinated that this lady could assemble such a large group of people and do collective bargaining and get resolutions on issues that were very crucial to our neighborhood.

However, among the few people who did not particularly appreciate my mother for such gatherings were her sons. My brothers and I always felt like she was giving more energy to the neighborhood friends than she was to us. Though I always respected my mother, I began to build a bit of resentment.

Just like my father, my mother was the type of person who was jolly to all people. She would throw her heart and soul into things as if they were her own issues and problems. I really appreciated that about my mother. Everyone knew they had a true friend in her, especially when facing tough issues. She's absolutely genuine. She could let her hair down to the ground, pull up a seat, look you straight in the eyes, and talk to you until all that negative energy is sucked right out of you and you're ready to walk away as a new person.

My mother is a spiritual motivator. Something about her touches you inwardly. She could go into a roomful of stars and they'll all come out saying, "Wow! Do you know this doctor, Lorraine Johnson? She's dynamite!" I've seen her work that magic on numerous occasions. I just sit back and say, "That's my mother."

Once my mother learned of my addiction to drugs, I believe our relationship went to a different level. I think she finally felt powerless. At the time of my writing this book, I'm anxiously waiting to read her portion so that I may get her point of view. My preference was to wait and read it once the book was done.

I imagine she was feeling helpless back then. She could counsel anyone else in the world experiencing tremendous heartache, but she could not circumvent the pain that she felt as a mom. Could she manage the lack of power and control she felt as a codependent with respect to her own son being a drug addict and alcoholic? A part of me felt that this was finally something that she and I could sit down and come to grips with and have her not be the expert. In a strange way I appreciated being in a position to school her on the subject of addiction recovery and what it was really all about.

It seemed to me that my mom gave more attention and nurturing to my middle and younger brothers. This bothered me to a great degree because I didn't understand it. Perhaps she felt I was self-sufficient or on the right track so I didn't need her guidance. I am not really sure. She would just kind of pass her words of wisdom, love, understanding and guidance over me. It appeared she would give her emotions to my siblings. I need to be very honest about this. It frankly put a significant strain on our relationship.

That strain turned into resentment and animosity throughout my using days, and set up an environment for disappointment and pain in many aspects of my life. I just said to myself that it was my turn to have an issue. I wanted her attention. I wanted her to focus on me! It was something I carried through my addiction.

Overall I am very fortunate to have a mother like her: A mother with whom I can sit down and agree to write a book concerning the things we were feeling at that screwed up time in our lives. I hope this book brings us closer. We are very much alike. It will be interesting if, because of this project and our mutual desire to help others, she and I travel together from one group to the next speaking and sharing our experience.

As she reads this book, I want her to know that I have always had not only unconditional love for her, but also great respect and admiration. She is very highly regarded in my mind, soul and spirit. I love you, mom.

Sheryl Johnson fills many important roles for me. She is my lover, my best friend, my "homie," my spirit, my connection, my wife, and the mother of my children. She is a remarkable woman.

Feisty and a go-getter, my wife sometimes reminds me of my mother. The sky's the limit in terms of their potential. I first met Sheryl when I was nineteen years old, on my birthday, through mutual friends. She was an incoming freshman at Texas Southern University. I had already been there for about a year. We befriended each other and sort of hung out and "kicked it" before deciding we liked each other enough to seriously date, get engaged, and then schedule a wedding date. But we went through a lot along the way.

To this day, she claims that I never properly asked her to marry me, but I don't know if that's true or not. However, I do know that I've definitely been given the most beautiful fourteen years of marriage that I think any man could ask for. And she was with me through my complete wreckage. She was there for me in every sense of the way. She was by my side and she saw me bottom out. To this day we never talk about that "bottom." I don't know how she dealt with it.

When I was taken away from campus and put into the treatment facility for thirty days and couldn't have visitors, Sheryl and I would talk on the phone every night. While I was in treatment, we became closer. We said things to each other that we had never said before. We didn't have to see each other to fully connect. We spoke over the phone and connected spiritually.

Back then when we were so young, Sheryl placed an ultimatum on me. She said, "You can't keep walking in and out of the doors of alcoholism and drug addiction thinking I'm always going to be here for you. When you decide to come home, you're going to have to make a decision. Don't make it for me. Make it for you. I have to let you know, I will get on with my life without you if you can't stay sober."

Those powerful words echoed in my mind. I mean, Wow! That was one of the most profound statements that anyone made to me during my recovery. She definitely had my attention. I took that into great consideration, among other things, and decided to stay drug and alcohol free. I appreciate her for giving me an ultimatum.

What I really enjoyed during the early part of my recovery was that we spent a lot of quality time together. We went to dollar movies, ate out at cheap restaurants and played a lot of dominoes. She shared a house in Houston with two other young women. We would just close her door and entertain each other. We really grew close. She knew I was scared. I was like a little bird that couldn't fly away from its nest because my wings weren't strong enough. She was there with her hands outstretched saying, "If you attempt to fly, I'll be here to catch you if you fall."

I really appreciated her love and loyalty as I attempted to get a handle on my addictions. I can't say enough about her being there. Black people know couples don't usually stay together under intense circumstances like these. But we did. It definitely can be done. We stuck together through the thick of the thick, the bottom of the bottom. Becoming each other's refuge, we watched each other grow from there. I would like to say to my soul mate, Sheryl Johnson, "I love you with all my heart. I give you the greatest of respect. I will do anything for you. Thank you so much for being there for me."

My younger brother, Randolph Lamont Johnson, I love and hate at the same time. I love him to death and that's the problem. With Randolph being three years younger, I remember always protecting him and cleaning up his mess behind him. As I went into recovery, it took a little time before it dawned on him that I was in very real and very serious trouble. He viewed me as a sort of closet role model in that he began to dibble and dabble in mind-altering chemicals himself.

Seeing my addiction get the best of me, Randy went into a tailspin because he realized he was going down the same path. He thought his older brother was hip, slick, and cool. Consequently, he almost lost me as a result of this drug addiction. He did not know how to stop his addiction right away. At this point in our lives, some resentment built between us.

He failed his first attempt in his recovery process. This is not unusual, but he never got serious about his recovery even after that. It hurts me to my heart. I finally had to let him know how I felt about his recovery process and leave the rest in God's hands. Randy has been coddled and protected pretty much all of his life. I would like to say to him, "I just love you, my brother and I haven't given up on you, man. I believe in your recovery. I believe you can and will do it. You must do it for Randy and you must stay true to yourself. I hope and wish the best for you. I'm always here for you."

Rashad Adrian Johnson, my youngest brother, is always the one, out of all of us, who really has his act together. He was "all that and a bowl of chips," as they say. Rashad was an outstanding kid, straight-A student, high-quality athlete, who just seemed to do everything the right way. He saw Randy and I go through a lot with addictions and decided he wasn't going to put himself through any of it. That's the thing that I appreciate about Rashad. He made up his mind and he simply stayed straight.

Not only did Rashad say no to the illness of drug and alcohol addiction for himself, he also thought of our parents. He did not want to put them through this torment. He felt both he and our parents deserved better than that. Therefore, he set himself up to achieve by studying hard, keeping his act clean and making great efforts to do the right thing. He is almost finished college and I feel confident that he will stay on the right path. I feel confident he'll stay drug and alcohol free.

To Rashad I say, "I am so proud of you!" My heart bubbles over with pride for him. I don't say much to him, nor do I give him a lot of accolades, but he is definitely one of my silent heroes. I have an abundance of respect for him. I expect much bigger and better things from and for him in his life. I love him tremendously. I will do anything in my power to help him.

Then there's Rudolph A. Johnson IV, my son, Little Rudy, who is the reason I live, breathe, work, make sacrifices and do all that I do. I'm just in love with the kid. Of course, this is natural for any parent to say, but there was a point in my time that I didn't even love myself. To be able to say in my recovery that I love myself and love my family is a miracle and a blessing.

My son adds so much spice, so much joy to my life. He is absolutely an inspiration for me. Sure, at times he wears me out, as children are so capable of doing, but that is my boy. Readers can understand that any eleven-year old will wear your patience and energy down, but we bounce right back the next day and go with the flow. That's what parenting is all about. It's been a great experience so far.

One of the things that Sheryl and I decided, before becoming parents, was that we wanted our children to grow up in a drug and alcohol-free environment. We had an opportunity to do that, one day at a time, with the assistance of our Higher Power.

Every now and then when I take a moment to smoke a cigar, Rudy will say, "Daddy, you're not suppose to smoke a cigar, it's bad for your health." It just sends me into shivers. I put the cigar out and say to him, "You're right, man. You're right." So, I couldn't even imagine him witnessing me taking a hit off a joint, snorting a line or drinking any kind of liquor. It's just not in the equation. Through God's good will, I hope to continue to be a positive role model for my son.

Then there is Mallory, my beautiful five-year-old daughter. Mallory is also my heart and soul. When I walk through the door at night, she is the first one to come running to put her arms around me. She shows she loves her father, and I love her.

My son and daughter keep me on task daily, motivating me to remain on the straight and narrow.

CHAPTER VI

MOTHER: LETTING GO AND LETTING GOD

SON: REBUILDING MY LIFE

MOTHER: LETTING GO AND LETTING GOD

Moving out of our house was like having a ten-ton bag of bricks lifted off my shoulders. I felt instant relief. No questions, no "what ifs." It was difficult, but there was no doubt in my mind that it was the right thing to do. All of those years, experiencing the daily tension of living in a lie, pretending all was well, had come to an abrupt halt. We were all in pain, hurt, confused, wishing it could have worked out, but collectively at peace with the truth.

During this time, I focused on learning everything I could about substance abuse, dysfunctional families and relationships, and codependency. I remained in therapy and worked on personal emotional baggage.

I had to revolutionize my very essence after I realized that co-dependent enabling was my disease. I had to go on a long journey of self examination, explore my every emotion, revisit my childhood storms, evaluate personal and social interaction, replay and embrace my unfulfilled needs, tear down my false sense of pride, dismantle my self-identity mask and look under every nook and cranny for people, places and things that invited me to retreat from reality.

I had to search through the wreckage of my personal life, and when I uncovered half-truths and downright lies, it caused me to pause and rendered me into emotional bondage. I had to force myself to keep going, daring myself, pushing myself, dragging myself toward the light of truth and reality.

Oh how I longed for the safety of my codependency. Oh how I yearned to remain in that sacred role. However, my unconditional love for my first-born child to be saved and gain back his sobriety required me to take that long hard look at the woman in the mirror. That was a very scary image for me to face. For the first time in my life facing my codependency allowed me to take the time to look at my inner self and make a commitment for positive self-change. The ultimate wreckage of a full-blown codependent is the creation of the "perfect" dysfunctional family built on false pride and shaky self-identity.

All my childhood secrets had to be dealt with and totally dismantled. I did not know what I would find hidden, waiting underneath this mask of what I referred to as a self-identity overlay.

I had to work through my anger with my biological father, forgiving him for abandoning me and for his failure to protect me. In addition to forgiving him, I worked on understanding why he was emotionally and physically unable to be a parent/father.

I was eventually able to work through, forgive and understand my ex-husband for his inability to make a commitment to monogamy. I came to understand and accept our mutual strengths, weakness, and our emotional baggage.

So, for the first time in my life, I found myself at peace, relaxed, taking life one day at a time, trusting the process, willing to experience the day-to-day parallel dimensions of life. I no longer needed to brace myself for unseen forthcoming disasters. It was not necessary to plan the role of codependent. I came to the understanding that I am a caring, sensitive, compassionate woman, mother, neighbor and friend. I was able to take better care of myself, as well as understand the need to set boundaries for the people I love. I was able to understand and appreciate that saying "no" did not mean you rejected or abandoned someone, but that no is sometimes an appropriate and necessary response.

Being able to set boundaries gave my family and children an opportunity to develop and internalize their own ability to problem-solve, and to find positive alternative solutions. Most importantly, it gave them the confidence to know that they could make their own successful decisions.

I am not going to say it was easy. I still catch myself in relapse, having the craving to rescue. But now I am able to self assess, understand where the desire and need comes from, and reframe my thinking and actions.

I am now able to laugh at myself for having a codependent thought. I can encourage, give out positive recovery information and support, yet accept that I'm powerless to all outcomes. Today, I can finally say, I have found and vanquished my personal demons and that I choose not to live in guilt, shame or fantasy.

I am able to face the truth and reality, no matter how difficult it may be. I know that each day I must trust in my Higher Power for guidance, understanding, wisdom and peace. I'm not saying my life is perfect. It was insane to believe that if I controlled everything, pretended that all was well, did everything for everybody, then everything would be perfect.

So, to my son Rudolph A. Johnson III, I must ask for your forgiveness for not giving you all the attention and support you needed. For treating you like a superstar instead of like my firstborn son who needed his mother's love just as much as his younger brothers.

I hope I have learned to balance my role as your mother, guide and friend.

I want to tell you how sorry I am for not giving you your fair share of nurturing and attention during my codependent addiction. I pray for your freedom from a codependent support system and from a mother who was so paralyzed, entrenched, engulfed and gripped by her disease, that she couldn't recognize yours.

I love you and I hope we can continue our healing and renew our friendship, as we help others in this life-long journey.

Son: Rebuilding My Life

Rebuilding my life is all about surrendering. The reason I say "surrendering" is because I can still recall the night I made that decision to "surrender" my life back to my Higher Power. The very next day I attended an AA meeting. I sat in the back of the room, once again, at the Post Oak Club.

It was during that meeting that I vowed to surrender to my Higher Power, to do what I couldn't do for myself. I also made the decision to follow the directions, rules and regulations of the Twelve-Step Program. For far too long I attempted to recover on my own, using my set of rules and regulations.

This time was different. Not only was I battered and beaten, feeling sick and tired of being sick and tired, but I was completely ready to relinquish all control to my Higher Power. It was time to get gut-level honest with myself with respect to who I was, and always will be – a recovering drug addict and alcoholic.

I had been neglecting some very important aspects of my life. I began failing in the pursuit of my personal goals, dreams and aspirations in my life, and I was not giving proper attention to personal hygiene, appearance, and how I presented myself in public. Everything about me was below par. I had to start all over again at building myself up from ground zero.

I commenced to shave, groom my hair, wear clean clothes and make sure I was always neat and presentable. This was necessary for cleaning up my physical environment, but more importantly, my spiritual environment. I wanted to be acceptable again around positive upwardly-mobile people. This was a major part of surrendering to my healing process.

The advice of my sponsor, William A., made a strong impression on me. I prioritized my list of ten things that I needed to do, but least wanted to do. My lowest priority became my highest priority. It became my motivation and assisted me with self-discipline. Since that moment, until today, I have continued to do it on a daily basis. It allows me to be a self-motivated person, making me reach deeper and work harder to reach my goals. Most of all, I was proving to myself that I could overcome and recover from the illness of crack cocaine addiction and alcohol abuse.

This is the key factor I want to share with those individuals hooked on crack cocaine. Too often, we feel our struggles are hopeless. We do not have that fulfilling environment surrounding us with people who have overcome this particular hurdle and who can provide us the example of long-term sobriety. The hurdle of overcoming the abuse of crack cocaine is so difficult that the inability to jump off it can be paralyzing. The mere thought of not knowing whether we can get over it is cause enough to send an abuser into a severe relapse.

Self-discipline, following the rules and regulations of the Twelve-Step Program and surrendering to a Higher Power is extremely crucial to get over the hurdle. Once making it over, life is triumphant on the other side.

If we don't begin the process to get over that initial hurdle, we will never know what beauty there is in a life of sobriety, being free of the chains of an addiction, to be who you really are and do some wonderful things with your life.

There is a life after crack cocaine addiction. Most users think abusing drugs is the most thrilling event in life because the euphoria of this type of drug is so overwhelming. A user believes that no other aspect of life can achieve that feeling.

The real reality is the feeling of being able to handle your own day-to-day business and feeling good about yourself. It is the true euphoria of life itself. We fail to realize that being surrounded by a loving family and putting the pieces of our lives back together is more powerful than the high of any synthetic drug. And so is the awesome feeling of assisting another person in the journey through the recovery process.

There are simply no words that can adequately describe the "high" from such an experience. When I speak to young adults at junior high and high schools, I explain to them their lack of understanding of what recovery is truly all about. I explain to them that they will not understand until they, themselves, have experienced turning their soul inside out, shaking it, then stuffing it back inside their body to start life anew.

I discuss with these youths that feeling of emptiness inside, an emptiness of all the negative substances and actions previously participated in on the streets. The emptiness yields to a feeling of cleanliness, a cleanliness that allows the ex-abuser to begin refilling his life with new, more positive aspects. This is an extremely important aspect in understanding the recovery process.

Without this experience of emptying out, one will not really be able to comprehend what recovery entails. This is why individuals who have not gone through the process and attempt to talk to recovering addicts and alcoholics often get a lot of flack. One simply cannot understand until one has actually gone through the whole process. It's as basic as that.

This is one of the main reasons I decided to write this book. I can totally relate to what a recovering addict is facing because I have been there and still work on it in my daily life, one day at a time. I can honestly tell you that recovery is possible, if you decide to do so.

I would like to point out the importance of being willing to freely share your emotions. For many of us, this is a very difficult task. Again, I am here to tell you, it can be done if you so choose.

I had to learn to get in touch with my own emotions. As a user, I basically numbed my emotions. I did not know what love was, what pain was or what being truly happy in a fulfilling environment was. I did not understand how special my relationships, with friends and family, really were.

This all had to be relearned as I became sober. It's like being a baby again, learning to feel those emotions all over again, but this time as a sober individual. This is an important key to long-term sobriety because in the days of using, when those emotions were felt, they were quickly cut off by a hit on a joint, a drink of alcohol, a toot of cocaine or whatever your drug of choice. The abuse of the substance was for the very purpose of numbing your feelings and emotions, whether good or bad. Being sober, the numbness is no longer there and emotions are often raw.

A major change in my first year of sobriety, and an important factor to long-term sobriety, is recognizing feeling those emotions. For instance, in those days, I began to grow closer to my girlfriend, now my wife. I remember having long discussions with her that I was unable to handle before. In my using days, sitting down in conversation for any length of time was close to impossible. Long discussions were unheard of.

By learning to relate to my emotions, conversations were much more rewarding, fulfilling and uplifting. We would just talk and talk and talk. It was very new to me because I had never enjoyed that type of intimacy outside of my family.

I learned to love and appreciate other individuals, to value them for assisting me in the process of my recovery, for being there when I needed them. They were there from their hearts. Their help was genuine. The friends I thought would ridicule, make fun of, and get angry with me, were the friends who supported me all the way. They were a source of great encouragement.

Yes, that too. I had to learn how to accept encouragement and help. I had to learn how to take being nurtured and reciprocate it. My friends and I have put the past behind us. At the same time, it is due to the past that our friendships are that much stronger today. To this very day I can call on any one of them and know they will be there for me and I for them because the friendship, the love and the trust is there.

A piece of me had to be given back to those individuals who supported me during my illness and during all the negative, unacceptable behaviors of that time in my life. I address this further in the Q and A chapter where I speak of the things my family and I are making an effort to do in order to give back and reach out. As they say in the Twelve-Step Program, "to twelve-step my fellow addicts and alcoholics that are still out there using, to assist them to come into the world of recovery and out of the dark, cold world of using."

In retrospect, perhaps I finally reached my true bottom when I was truly done with being sick and tired and was ready to accept friendships and emotions. I was just plain ready, in my heart and soul, to do whatever it took to begin my journey and to ensure that, this time around, I would succeed in sobriety.

I became humble and patient. I didn't try to over-talk anyone or try to invent my own laws or supercede the rules of the Twelve-Step Program. I sat back and listened and played by the rules of the game. I finally found something that worked for Rudy. This meant doing some things different than before and having a different kind of relationship with my sponsor.

I learned to be open to suggestions that were comfortable for me.

Not all suggestions work for everyone, but we must learn to be open to those that may work for us as individuals. I began reading the "Big Book," the Holy Bible. There may be another book that works for you; it's a very personal choice. For me, it was the Bible.

I commenced writing through the steps on paper as a sort of cleansing. This was very helpful to get rid of the emotional "baggage" and "trash" out of my system, releasing the "poison." This meant being willing to fight a good fight, being willing to go to the end of your rope, as in your using days, but in an opposite direction, attacking your recovery process in the same aggressive manner.

Recovery will happen. Your world will come to you. The promises in the Big Book will start to unveil themselves to you. You will begin reaping all the benefits and good things in life that other recovery individuals have achieved. This is no mystery, these aren't just words written by someone with no experience with this particular issue. This is a recovering drug addict and alcoholic talking to you who has gone through this particular ritual, now living life in sober wisdom.

One of the things I so wanted to do was put together one full year of sobriety. I remember making that particular deal with myself. Then one year led to another and another. I found that life was much better sober than as an addict. I will take one day living sober over twenty-three days of practicing the use of alcohol and drugs.

I really enjoyed putting the pieces of my life back together again. My family became closer. I began to understand my relationships better. I understand when I need to back away from them and to allow them some room to breathe. They, in turn, understand when to back away from me and to give me the same consideration. We know the love is there, the bond is there and it will always remain strong.

A big lesson for me was experiencing adult love for the first time in my life. I learned how to love a woman, a woman who is now my wife, Sheryl.

We now have two healthy, strong-willed children, eleven-year-old Rudy IV, and five-year-old Mallory. We understand the love we have for each other as well as the love we mutually have for our children.

I have been able, through my Higher Power, to give some of this love back, not only to the community of people who produced me, but also to the recovery community (those individuals who are in recovery or those who are on the outside waiting to jump into recovery). Those positive things are what I hoped and wished for while I was struggling with my own recovery process.

One other note before I end is the fact that I understand that I was very, very, very fortunate. Not everyone recovers from alcoholism and drug addiction. There have been many tragic deaths. Many individuals have been placed into institutions, both lockup and mental institutions where they must be treated on a daily basis.

This is why I wanted to tell my story. I wanted to give it away. I had to release it in order to get it back, believing that doing this will benefit those who need to hear a story of addiction and successful recovery. I hope that some of the things that I revealed will be of benefit. I hope you understand that this recovery process is not hopeless; that you will learn to appreciate the things an individual has to go through on their road to recovery. I hope you will never forget where you have come from, and when you get to recovery, that you remember to turn around and give it back.

One of my dreams is to be able to assist young people as they struggle through the pain and suffering of the illness of addiction. What I decided in the second year of my sobriety was to set up a program that could help save young people from this devastating drug and alcohol epidemic. We are losing too many young people to the street, to drug and alcohol abuse. I was almost lost – now I want to be there to help.

CHAPTER VII

TOGETHER

MOTHER & SON
Q & A

CHAPTER VII

This chapter is a series of probing questions and revealing answers from both mother and son.

We hope these personal revelations about addiction will give additional insight to help you along your recovery journey.

Q & A: MOTHER

Q: *Dr. Johnson, did you see yourself as the person to pull your child away from this sickness?*

A: I think Rudy's response was perfect about "saving" because our family never had experience with how to build an alcohol and drug recovery model. We have generations of alcohol and drug addicts we just accepted as having normal lifestyles. I don't know how to say it any better than that except that we all had family members who were active alcohol and drug addicts, but we saw it as acceptable.

As a result, when Rudy called and said that he was in trouble with alcohol and drugs, first of all, we were in shock. No, no one could believe that Rudy was an alcoholic and a drug addict. He was so functional and successful in college. He was almost in his senior year, he looked the part, he wasn't homeless, he wasn't begging. We saw him as a successful person. So, we just figured alcohol and drugs, now what can we do? Let's get him a little help and he'll jump right back on his feet and everything will be cool.

We didn't see it as him being in the bowels of a disease. We saw him as a successful person who could handle anything that was dealt to him. That was the biggest misconception. We always expected Rudy to be number one, the first, the gusto, the leader. And even after acknowledging his addiction, we expected him to pick himself up, dust himself off and get back in the race.

We didn't have a clue, even as clinicians, myself a therapist. Being emotionally involved, I did not have a clue. I did not personally know what codependency was in itself, what my codependency role was, or what alcohol and drug dependency was as a disease – because it was an accepted part of life for us. My father was an alcoholic, but he was functional until he died. I just figured alcoholics and addicts go on until they get well.

I did not understand it was a process, a program, a twelve-step program that you work one day at a time, and that you have to embrace this program that turns your life inside out. In the beginning we were just hopeless, powerless, depressed and panicked. At the same time, we wanted Rudy to get some help and get on his feet, but we really didn't see a connection between programs, our codependency and the whole scene. In that respect, I concur with Rudy in that we just couldn't see how we could save him. We did not think he needed saving. This was our capable Rudy. He was going to get it together and he was going to be all right.

Q: *As a mother, where was your releasing point pertaining to Rudy's sickness?*
A: What was the turning point for me? An important point to get to is where it doesn't matter how the person came to use drugs. Whether it was because they were around drugs and alcohol and their role models were getting high and drinking – or whether they had none of that at home and they had very good role models – or whether the family had double standards, making sure only non-drug type activities were visible.

Whichever scenario, the end product is always the same. The child becomes an alcoholic addict. The parents, particularly mothers, get caught off guard and it knocks them flat on their stomach and they cry out for mercy. You wrestle with it and you wrestle with it. You try to fix it. You try to pull in every resource. You call every number. You try to do everything that you can do. You even try to do everything beyond your power and you still get to the bottom line that you cannot change the alcoholic addict.

The turning point for me was realizing there's nothing I could do, except one thing, let go and let God. I know that may sound simplistic. I know the reader will say, "What do you mean, let go and let God? What is that?"
It's a process. It is something that you learn only by working the twelve steps relating to codependency. It is a spiritual quest that has nothing to do with how much money you have, how many degrees you have. It has nothing to do with your lifestyle, who you are, whether you are from a two-parent or single-parent home.

It is a spiritual walk. What I mean is that in the program they refer to your Higher Power, whom I call God. At some point, when you know you cannot do anything, you have to cry out to God. Tell God, "I'm turning this over to you because I love this person so much. I know I am just interfering and I don't know what to do."

It takes a miracle. Recovery is the miracle business. Turning it over to God was the turning point for me. It didn't mean throwing anyone away. It just meant that you were powerless until you got your own life together. You had to change your lifestyle, change your method of interacting with the addicted person.

Once it was given to God, faith had to come in, faith that God was working. God was helping them work the program. Prior to this, you can't eat, can't sleep, you can't think, you're depressed. When you turn it over to Him, you receive an inner peace. When you reach that inner peace, you know that you have given it to God. Then, you have to work with patience and trust in the process.

I learned a lot of astonishing things – the most important being that I was not in control. In fact, I was out of control. I had to look at my own shortcomings. I needed to turn Rudy over to God. I was powerless. I had to trust my Higher Power and let Him do the healing.

Q: *Did your codependence affect your position as a therapist?*
A: That's a difficult question. As a therapist, counselor or whatever term you want to use, you see yourself as wisely advising other people. In my therapist role, I intellectually understood the disease of alcohol and drugs, but I couldn't use my skills because this involved my family, making it emotional for me.

I just went into denial. It had been easy for me to deal with patients who were alcoholics or addicts, and to counsel people who were dealing with family members who were alcoholics or addicts. But when I found out my son was an alcoholic-addict I felt guilty immediately.

I remember thinking to myself, now here this was right under my nose and even though I knew what you do in front of kids, positive role modeling, all of that, somehow, I felt my household was exempt. When you are in the thick of something, you just have these double ways of thinking about it, double standards or a double philosophy. The therapist's son is not going to grow up and be an addict. Rather, the therapist's son is going to grow up and be successful.

When you are in the business of helping people and your family falls apart, you feel a tremendous amount of grief, shame and guilt because you can't help your own child. With grief on top of it you feel, after coming out of your denial, you could just take a brick and hit yourself because you didn't want to see it. You feel you could have done something in terms of intervention much earlier, but you chose not to see it. You chose not to see it because it was safe for your heart not to see it.

Denial is great. It protects you from pain. Nobody wants to be in pain. So, what do you do? You choose to live in la-la land. I call it "la-la land" because you are in Disneyland. Even though you see the rides are breaking down with people falling and getting hurt, you are still there selling tickets for the ride. So, you feel a tremendous amount of guilt along with the powerlessness.

Once you come to grips with the powerlessness, you have to forgive yourself for being in denial. That applies to everybody. The co-dependents as well as the addict have to forgive themselves and look at their fourth step of making a self-assessment and making amends. The same twelve steps apply.

We have to make our own amends and look at our own baggage and wreckage in order to try to rectify it. One of the ways we do this is to face the reality of codependency and denial. When we face denial, we have to be honest with ourselves and admit we are not perfect. The addict's not perfect. We're not perfect. The disease doesn't care what color you are, how much money you have, how much education, whatever. The disease of alcohol and drug addiction can strike anybody, in any household.

Q: *Do you think there is unequal substance abuse treatment in our society?*

A: Yes, unfortunately. Historically in our country, a substance abuser who has money, power and resources can always have access to treatment. What we have to do is make the treatment playing field even. There are federal guidelines that state that anyone who is suffering from the disease of alcoholism should be treated with equality and have open, equal access to treatment, because it is a disease. It is not a social illness. It is a physical, psychological disease.

Once it was defined as a disease, then treatment should be equally accessible. However, because of the disparity of social economics in this country, the kind of treatment the alcoholic or substance abuse receives depends on how much money and resources they have.

Those who lack financial and political resources do not have much in the way of programs available to them. They are further stigmatized when they resort to criminal activity and the judicial system penalizes with prison time. Hence, the profile of people doing prison time tends to be more Latino, African-American, minorities, and more women and poor people who don't have access to a good criminal defense system.

Q: *In your view, what is the most important thing about this book?*

A: One day a few years ago, I woke up from a nap with this vision from my Higher Power. It gave me the compelling idea that Rudy and I should write a book about his recovery, about substance abuse, my recovery from co-dependency, and all the trials and tribulations that went into our individual and collective recovery.

God gave us the idea for this book and the titles for the chapters. I think the most important thing about this book is that God is the real author.

Q & A: SON

Q: *Rudy, what is your perspective on the drug problem in America?*
A: The drug activity in our country is way out of control, particularly in the inner cities where it is an epidemic. You have individuals with idle time and little encouragement or incentive to do the right thing in life. They see their family, their friends in a community in a dilapidated state. One of the things you do when you have idle time is to take mind-altering chemicals to enhance your mood in those downtrodden circumstances. We have to fix the community and its social ills along with "battling" the drugs on the street.

Q: *Do you view drug use as a slow death? What can families do knowing that this is self-destructive for their family member?*
A: Yes, alcohol and drug use is a disease and often a death sentence if you are actively involved in using and abusing. We consider it suicide. Your life is going to become socially, emotionally unmanageable, and eventually, your disease is going to kill you.

You only have three choices: You are either going to die, go to jail or another institution, or take the road to recovery.

"What can families do about it?" I think the first thing is to understand that you are powerless to the outcome. The first thing people who are codependent want to do is go out and "fix it." You want to roll your sleeves up and annihilate drug deals and politically march for laws to remove the drug from the community.

While that has to go in line with everything else, the most immediate thing that you have to do is to deal with your own emotions and feelings. If you really want to help the addict and alcoholic – you must work with yourself first. That means looking at your codependency, looking at how you rescue, looking at how you perceive and help the person that you are involved with in terms of helping them cope.

The hardest thing to do is "nothing." I know that sounds crazy if you do nothing for the drug addict and alcoholic, and attend to yourself first. But when you get yourself together, you understand how the disease works. Then, and only then, can you help addicts get into recovery, organize against drug availability, help the legislature, change the law, etc.

Q: *Did you view your mother as someone who was trying to save or help you during your using days?*
A: I don't know if I would consider it "saving" because in my mind that means someone who is real familiar with the disease of alcoholism and addiction and has a handle on a recovery plan, and my mother did not. Like most things in my life, I was the first one that I knew of who got into the business of establishing a plan of recovery by accident, by falling into it. I was suffering from alcoholism and drug addiction, dually addicted. There was no experience in my family.

My parents were receptive to whatever I needed to do to make myself functional as a human being. If that meant establishing a plan of recovery, then they were supportive. I think the hard thing for everyone in the household at that time was not knowing how to make the first step. It wasn't familiar to anyone. That has been the story of my life – a lot of "firsts."

Being powerless over the recovery process added some confusion and misunderstanding to the entire family, including me. It wasn't a systematic plan aided by a recovery process. It was more of a situation where we discovered Alcoholics Anonymous and other twelve-step programs.

Both of my parents were supportive of that recovery process and even pushed me to become more self sufficient, but not fully understanding the totality of the disease and the recovery plan. Until you get into the "rooms" of recovery yourself, you don't really understand the plan of the recovery process and also, the importance of practicing the steps that it takes to be a recovering addict and alcoholic and function again as a member of society.

Q: *How do you view your children in respect to your experience with drug addiction and alcoholism?*
A: First of all, I guess I see myself as being kind of a lightning rod in that I hope I have fallen and recovered for everybody in the household. However, I would be able to deal with my children, if, God forbid, they came home one day and said, "Dad, I'm suffering from alcoholism or drug addiction."

We have chosen to show our children the option of not using alcohol and drugs. I witnessed a different scene in my childhood – relatives drinking and doing drugs at family functions, having a good time. That was the way we celebrated. It was the norm. None were the wiser when there were five, six and seven year-olds patterning their behavior after adults that they love, respect and cherish.

If I flip that over, I see my wife and I having family functions free of alcohol, free of drugs, free of the drama that went with having a drug and alcohol function. Drama always ensued around mind-altered recreation. It's not that we don't have drama today. Even with non-alcohol and non-drug functions, there may be drama, but there is less, and it is not out of control.

What my kids are seeing is that you can still have fun, you can still kick it with your family, you can still have good friendships, you can still celebrate holidays and special events – without the drugs and alcohol. My children are waking up not seeing drugs being used in our house. I mentioned before, it was nothing seeing my dad or a family member getting high in the house. My children don't see that.

If they learn how to use, it will be outside of the square footage of our home. I can't say it won't happen. All I am saying is that when it comes to a time in their lives when they might experiment, they will be able to grab a reference point in how they were raised. They will be able to say, "Wow, mom and dad didn't drink alcohol and use drugs at the house: Now I have a decision to make." I would hope that by example I have given my children an alternative way to live.

Q: *Who were the most important people to help you through your recovery process?*
A: The list is very long. In the most intimate circle are those I call the "usual suspects" – my parents, my future wife, guys that I went to school

with at Texas Southern, and in particular, some of my teammates and coaches who intervened on me and got me to the hospital.

Starting the recovery process, when you get introduced to the twelve-step program, is just the "beginning." You start to flush out some of the things that weren't going so well in your life; character defects, things that you can improve upon. The same usual suspects were there at every stage and are still very close to me even though I've established sixteen years of recovery. So, those usual suspects have not changed their face, their colors, or their characteristics from the day that they intervened until today.

Although many people helped me over the years, a few really stuck with me, including my football coach who initially drove me to the hospital. I appreciate him and also my sponsor, William A, who was there telling me that I could make it as I went in and out of the program several times. He pretty much guided me through my first year of sobriety. I never thought I could do a year. A year was a huge challenge for me. Three hundred sixty five days of nothing, of being clean and sober was something I couldn't even fathom in the beginning.

As time went on, I began to rely on my family and my wife a lot. My wife was the one who was there dealing with my ups and downs, my emotional swings. Even after a year or two, maybe three, of recovery you still have the same emotional patterns, you just do it dry. To this day, many years later, I'll go through an emotional swing and she'll say, "Hey, you need to check yourself because that's the same old addict behavior coming back."

I can't say enough about the guys who were on my football team because they had a choice at that point. When my addiction was revealed, they could have written me off as someone who was an outcast to society. We tend to discard individuals who don't fit in, nice and neat, with the status quo, discard them in jail or institutions and certainly cast them out of our social groups. When a person is cast out, it is not known if that individual was worth something. But these guys kept me in their social group and allowed me to recover. They waited it out until I was able to come around and become a contributing member of the group. Now I am a trusted and respected member of that group.

If they had kicked me off their team years ago, I could not have contributed later. Now I answer calls about children who are just being born. I give marital advice. I talk about the things I'm doing in the community and how they can pattern their own lives in the community. I am a listening ear sometimes in two-hour conversations between guys, which is unusual. Sixteen years ago, I could not be like that. I couldn't even be anything to myself.

The overriding message I would like to convey is the fact that when you admit that you are suffering from this disease, there is a possibility of recovery. Understand that you don't get cast out because you make that announcement. If nothing else, part of the reason for my writing this book is to tell you that you can and will recover if you do the right things that it takes to recover.

Not all of us make it to recovery, in particular, young African-Americans. We tend to be cast out, not only of our own little circle, but also out of society. A young African-American male or female with an addiction or alcohol problem – that's double jeopardy.

Q: *Do you have a better understanding of drug and alcohol addiction today versus sixteen years ago?*
A: I don't know if there is any better understanding of alcoholism and drug

addiction from the layperson's perspective. I think most people still think of drug addicts and alcoholics as bad, people they feel very uncomfortable around and want to keep their distance from.

Medical research into alcoholism and drug addiction has progressed leaps and bounds from fifteen or twenty years ago. However, until regular folk, who are the mothers, fathers, uncles, brothers and the "community," have a better understanding of what it takes to recover from alcoholism and drug addiction, we will lose people in this society. Individuals suffering from this illness will always be discarded. Until we can deal with medically treating these individuals, one day at a time, it's going to be tough reaching out and rescuing them.

Q: *What has had the most impact on helping people to recover in your community from alcohol and drug abuse?*
A: In every recovering alcoholic or addict's process, in line with the twelve steps, you are faced with the responsibility of giving back the gift of recovery. Years ago I made a decision, with the help of my wife, to organize, not run, an effort that would provide education and intervention at the elementary, junior high and high school level for inner-city children.

That decision was the birth of Pros and Coaches Anti-Drug Campaign. My wife and I decided that we wanted to do a three or four-day campaign to get the word out to inner-city children that: 1) drugs and alcohol can kill you and 2) if you did find that you or a family member were addicted, then there is help available through twelve-step recovery programs.

I designed the program to include some of my influential friends, ex-teammates and colleagues who were successful in doing some positive things around the country. I wanted to provide those inner-city kids in the back of the room who were quietly living in tough situations, with a connection to an alternate positive lifestyle.

I took to the mentoring. I got caught up in introducing kids who thought they had been forgotten by society to people who they could see on TV on any given Sunday, and who cared. I don't believe that one person can come out and tell a whole group of people to stay drug-free and that's all they need.

What you can do is start with that small touch, that gesture that says today the only important thing on my schedule is to make sure I get to your school on time, see your smiling face, leave you with a personal story, hug you, shake your hand, give you a kiss or an autograph. That's your special time, the most important thing on my schedule today. Inner-city children don't get that very often. That was the birth of Pros and Coaches for me. Since that time we've interfaced with well over ten thousand students. We've been to every single inner-city elementary, junior high and high school in and around San Diego County. We've given away over ten thousand dollars of scholarship money. We have children in college, those who have graduated and those who are about to go. We are gratified that there are individuals who feel like that touch, that gift that we brought has changed their life forever.

Then you ask yourself, what else can I do out there? My wife and I decided we would open up a new chapter of our life in recovery and try to assist the community get one step closer to understanding this very deadly disease of alcoholism and drug addiction. Pros and Coaches served two purposes. It helped me get involved with the community, and allowed me to retain, through my twelve steps, the energy and encouragement to continue to stay sober, one day at a time.

STATISTICS

STATISTICS AND INFORMATION ABOUT CRACK COCAINE AND ALCOHOL

Cocaine

Pure cocaine was first used in the 1880s as a local anesthetic in eye, nose, and throat surgeries because of its ability to provide anesthesia as well as to constrict blood vessels and limit bleeding. Many of its therapeutic applications are now obsolete due to the development of safer drugs. Approximately 100 years after cocaine entered into use, a new variation of the substance emerged. This substance, crack cocaine, became enormously popular in the mid-1980s due in part to its almost immediate high and the fact that it is inexpensive to produce and buy.

Traditionally, cocaine was a rich man's drug, due to the large expense of a cocaine habit. Now, crack cocaine is being sold at prices low enough that even adolescents can afford to buy it. But, this is misleading, since once a person is addicted to crack cocaine, his "habit" often increases, and so does his expense.

Crack Cocaine

Crack cocaine is a solid form of freebase cocaine. Crack cocaine is the street name given to one form of freebase cocaine that comes in small lumps or shavings. Freebase is the treatment of cocaine with chemicals, which frees the cocaine base from the hydrochloride and lowers the temperature at which the cocaine melts.

The term "crack" refers to the crackling sound heard when the mixture is smoked (heated), presumably from the sodium bicarbonate. One gram of pure powder cocaine will convert to approximately 0.89 grams of crack cocaine. The Drug Enforcement Administration estimates that crack cocaine rocks are between 75 and 90 percent pure cocaine.

Crack cocaine typically is smoked in pipes constructed of glass bowls fitted with one or more fine mesh screens that support the drug. The user heats the side of the bowl (usually with a lighter), and the heat causes the crack cocaine to vaporize. The user inhales the cocaine-laden fumes through the pipe. Facilitated by the large surface area of the lungs' air sacs, as crack cocaine is smoked it is absorbed almost immediately into the bloodstream, taking only 19 seconds to reach the brain.

Smoking remains the predominant route of crack cocaine administration. However, some sources indicate that crack cocaine is also sometimes injected or snorted. Snorting is the process of inhaling crack cocaine powder through the nose where it is absorbed into the bloodstream through the nasal tissues. Injecting is the act of using a needle to release the crack cocaine directly into the bloodstream.

In some cities, crack cocaine is combined with other substances and injected. For example, in Washington, D.C., it is reported that crack cocaine is combined with heroin and marijuana and then injected. Also, in New Orleans, crack cocaine is injected with heroin in a "speedball." Additionally, crack cocaine can be sprinkled in cigarettes or marijuana joints and smoked. These cocaine and crack cocaine-laced joints are referred to as "primos."

Crack Addiction

Crack addiction is a process that is both rapid and severe. Those who believe that their "recreational" use is under control are not immune from the threat of addiction. Clinicians estimate that 10 percent of recreational users will go on to serious, heavy use of cocaine.

Crack cocaine is a powerfully addictive drug of abuse. Once having tried crack cocaine, an individual cannot predict or control the extent to which he or she will continue to use the drug. Crack cocaine has become a major problem in many American cities because it is inexpensive – selling for between $5 and $10 for one or two doses (usually 300-500mg) – and easily transportable – sold in small vials, folding paper, or tinfoil.

Users who become addicted will "crave" more of the drug as soon as the intoxicating effects wear off, if they do not get their regular dose. Abusers may have a hard time limiting their use and may build a tolerance to the drug, requiring larger amounts to get the same desired effect. They may develop problems with schools, jobs, and personal relationships. Addicts have to support expensive habits, which can cause them to quickly turn to a life of crime: shoplifting, theft, drug dealing, and prostitution.

Attempts to stop using the drugs can fail simply because the resulting depression can be overwhelming, causing the addict to use more cocaine in an attempt to overcome his depression. This overpowering addiction can cause the addict to do anything to get cocaine. Recent studies on cocaine and addiction have shown that, during periods of abstinence from cocaine use, the memory of the euphoria associated with cocaine, or mere exposure to cues associated with cocaine use, can trigger tremendous craving and relapse to cocaine, even after long periods of abstinence.

Researchers have found that cocaine stimulates the brain's reward system inducing an even greater feeling of pleasure than natural functions. In turn, its influence on the reward circuit can lead a user to bypass survival activities and repeat drug use. Chronic cocaine use can lead to a cocaine addiction and in some cases damage the brain and other organs. An addict will continue to use cocaine even when faced with adverse consequences.

Health Hazards of Cocaine Use

Cocaine is a strong central nervous system stimulant that interferes with the re-absorption process of dopamine, a chemical messenger associated with pleasure and movement. Dopamine is released as part of the brain's reward system and is involved in the high that characterizes cocaine consumption.

Physical effects of cocaine use include constricted peripheral blood vessels, dilated pupils, and increased temperature, heart rate, and blood pressure. The duration of cocaine's immediate euphoric effects, which include hyper-stimulation, reduced fatigue, and mental clarity, depends on the route of administration. The faster the absorption, the more intense the high. On the other hand, the faster the absorption, the shorter the duration of action. The high from snorting may last 15 to 30 minutes, while that from smoking may last 5 to 10 minutes. Increased use can reduce the period of stimulation.

Some users of cocaine report feelings of restlessness, irritability, and anxiety. An appreciable tolerance to the high may be developed, and many addicts report that they seek but fail to achieve as much pleasure as they did from their first exposure. Scientific evidence suggests that the powerful neuropsychological reinforcing property of cocaine is responsible for an individual's continued use, despite harmful physical and social consequences. In rare instances, sudden death can occur on the first use of cocaine or unexpectedly thereafter. However, there is no way to determine who is prone to sudden death.

High doses of cocaine and/or prolonged use can trigger paranoia. Smoking crack cocaine can produce a particularly aggressive paranoid behavior in users. When addicted individuals stop using cocaine, they often become depressed. This also may lead to further cocaine use to alleviate depression. Prolonged cocaine snorting can result in ulceration of the mucous membrane of the nose and can damage the nasal septum enough to cause it to collapse. Cocaine-related deaths are often a result of cardiac arrest or seizures followed by respiratory arrest.

Cocaine Statistics

1 out of 4 Americans between the age of 26 and 34 have used cocaine in their lifetime.

According to the Minnesota Institute for Public Health and drug prevention resource center, 5,000 adults in the United States try cocaine for the first time each day.

Regarding the ease by which one can obtain crack cocaine, 24.4% of 8th graders, 30.6% of 10th graders, and 40.2% of high school seniors surveyed in 2001 reported that crack cocaine was "fairly easy" or "very easy" to obtain.

According to the 2001 National Household Survey on Drug Abuse, approximately 6.2 million (2.8 percent) Americans age 12 or older had tried crack cocaine at least once in their lifetime, 1.0 million (0.5 percent) used crack cocaine in the past year, and 406,000 (0.2 percent) reported past month crack cocaine use.

Today it is estimated that 22 to 25 million people have tried cocaine at least once. Conservative estimates indicate that there are over two million cocaine addicts in the United States today.

Contrary to earlier belief high dose use of cocaine can be detected as long as 10 to 22 days after last use.

Near half of all drug-related emergency room visits are due to cocaine abuse.

Rates of cocaine use by college students over the previous 5 years has increased from 2.0% of all students in 1994 to 4.8% in 2000.

Cocaine use among men is almost twice that of women. The office of National Drug Control Policy estimates the number of chronic cocaine users at 3.6 million.

Adults 18 to 25 years of age currently have the highest percentage of cocaine use than any other age group.

90% of cocaine users smoked, drank, or used marijuana before trying cocaine.

Alcohol Abuse

Alcohol is the number one drug problem in America. Each year a typical young person in the United States is inundated with more than 1,000 commercials for beer and wine coolers and several thousand fictional drinking incidents on television. Each year the liquor industry spends 2 billion dollars on advertising and encouraging the consumption of alcoholic beverages.

Alcohol is a sedative-hypnotic with a tranquilizing effect. Almost all the alcohol you drink is absorbed rapidly from the stomach or small intestines, reaching the brain within five minutes.

Though the FDA ironically lists it as a food, alcohol has no significant nutrients, vitamins or minerals, and is mainly empty calories. From a health standpoint, alcohol should be regarded as a nonprescription drug legally available to anyone of drinking age.

When people mix cocaine and alcohol consumption, they are compounding the danger each drug poses and unknowingly forming a complex chemical experiment within their bodies. NIDA-funded researchers have found that the human liver combines cocaine and alcohol and manufactures a third substance, coca ethylene, that intensifies cocaine's euphoric effects, while possibly increasing the risk of sudden death.

There is no cure for alcoholism, but various therapies can improve the situation and your life. The success of any treatment or program or medication depends on the patient's motivation, and support by family and friends.

Alcohol Statistics

43% of Americans have been exposed to alcoholism in their families.

Nearly 14 million Americans—one in every 13 adults—have a drinking problem, and approximately 500,000 are between the age of 9 and 12.

Americans spend over $90 billion total on alcohol each year.

An average American may consume over 25 gallons of beer, 2 gallons of wine, and 1.5 gallons of distilled spirits each year.

Each year students spend $5.5 billion on alcohol, more then they spend on soft drinks, tea, milk, juice, coffee, or books combined.

56% of students in grade 5 to 12 say that alcohol advertising encourages them to drink.

6.6% of employees in full-time jobs report heavy drinking, defined as drinking five or more drinks per occasion on five or more days in the past 30 days.

The highest percentage of heavy drinkers (12.2%) is found among unemployed adults between the ages of 26 to 34.

Up to 40% of all industrial fatalities and 47% of industrial injuries can be linked to alcohol consumption and alcoholism.

In 2000, almost 7 million persons age 12 to 20 were binge drinkers; that is, about one in five persons under the legal drinking age was a binge drinker.

Alcohol and alcohol-related problems are costing the American economy at least $100 million in health care and loss of productivity every year. 80% of problem drinkers are employed.

Four in ten criminal offenders report alcohol as a factor in violence.

Among spouse violence victims, three out of four incidents were reported to have involved alcohol use by the offender.

The 2001 survey shows 25 million (one in ten) Americans surveyed reported driving under the influence of alcohol. This report is nearly three million more than the previous year. Among young adults age 18 to 25 years, almost 23% drove under the influence of alcohol.

In the United States, every 30 minutes someone is killed in an alcohol-related traffic accident.

According to the National Institute on Alcohol Abuse and Alcoholism (NIAAA), alcohol is implicated in 50% of all homicides, 50% of all fatal auto accidents, 41% of all crimes, 33% of all suicides, and a large proportion of drowning, boat, and aircraft deaths.

Do you have a drinking or drug problem?

Ask yourself:

Have you ever felt you should cut down on your drinking or drug use?

Have people annoyed you by criticizing your drinking or drug use?

Have you ever felt bad or guilty about your drinking or drug habits?

Have you ever had a drink or taken recreational drugs first thing in the morning?

At least one "yes" suggests a possible alcohol or drug problem, and we urge you to seek additional screening and help.

RESOURCES

WE WANTED THIS BOOK TO BE MORE THAN A SHARING OF OUR STORY. WE ALSO WANTED TO OFFER YOU AN OPPORTUNITY TO KEEP THIS BOOK AS A RECOVERY REFERENCE GUIDE FOR YOUR FAMILY, FRIENDS AND MEMBERS OF THE COMMUNITY.

WE FEEL THAT KNOWLEDGE AND INFORMATION EQUALS FREEDOM, HEALING AND PEACE OF MIND.

WHEN YOU ARE FACED WITH A PERSONAL CRISIS, OR THE CRISIS OF A LOVED ONE, IT IS ENCOURAGING TO KNOW THAT HELP IS AVAILABLE THROUGH OUR HIGHER POWER, AND THROUGH COMMUNITY RECOVERY AND TREATMENT RESOURCES.

PLEASE KEEP THIS BOOK HANDY AS A RESOURCE GUIDE FOR YOU AND FOR THOSE YOU LOVE AND SERVE.

**P.S. REMEMBER THE AUTHORS OF THIS BOOK
ARE A TELEPHONE CALL AWAY:
1-800-970-3050**

RESOURCE AND REFERRAL LIST

Recovery Programs and Hotlines

AA: Chapter numbers are listed in your local telephone directory.
AA San Diego: 1-619 265-8762
NA: Narcotics Anonymous/Fellowship Services: 1-800-863-2962
CA: Cocaine Anonymous: 1-800-347-8998
Adolescent Suicide Hotline: 1-800-621-4000
Alcohol and Drug Helpline: 1-800-821-4357
Alcohol Drug and Treatment Referrals: 1-800-454-8966
Al-Anon/Alateen Family: 1-888-425-2666
Call for a child in immediate danger: 1-800-843-5678
Center for Substance Abuse Prevention (CSAP): 1-800-729-6686
Child Abuse National Hotline: 1-800-252-2873
Covenant House Hotline (runaways): 1-800-999-9999
Domestic Violence Hotline: 1-800-799-7233
Elder Abuse Hotline: 1-800-252-8966
Families Anonymous: 1-800-736-9805
Friends of Battered Women and Their Children: 1-800-603-4357
Hazelden Foundation: 1-800-257-7810
Institute of Mental Health Information: 1-800-647-2642
NAPARE Alcohol, Drug and Pregnancy: 1-800-368-BABY (2229)
National Alliance for the Mentally Ill: 1-800-950-6264
National Council on Alcoholism and Drug Dependence, Inc.: 1-800-622-2255
National Council on Alcohol and Drugs: 1-800-475-HOPE
National Drug Hotline [bi-lingual]: 1-800-662-4357; Spanish: 800-662-9832

National Inhalant Prevention Coalition: 1-800-269-4237

Runaway Hotline: 1-800-231-6946

Suicide Hotline: 1-800-784-2433

United Way of America: 1-800-411-8929

Youth Crisis Hotline: 1-800-442-4673

Recommended Books

Stepping Stones to Recovery, (paperback), *Bill Pittman*

The Thinking Person's Guide to Sobriety, *Bert Pluymen*

Twelve Steps and Twelve Traditions, (hardcover), *AA World Service Office*

Another Chance: Hope and Health for the Alcoholic Family,
     Sharon Wegschedider-Cruse

Codependent No More, (hardcover), *Melody Beattie*

Understanding the Twelve Steps: A Guide for Counselors, Therapists,
     and Recovering People, (paperback), *Terence Gorski*

Denial is Not a River in Egypt, (paperback), *Sandi Bachom, Don Ross*

Of Course You're Angry: A Guide to Dealing with the Emotions of
     Substance Abuse, (paperback), *Gayle Rosellini*

The Language of Letting Go, (hardcover, paperback), *Melody Beattie*

Our Children are Alcoholics: Coping with Children Who Have Addictions,
     (paperback), *Sally and David B.*

No is a Complete Sentence: Learning the Sacredness of Personal Boundaries,
     (paperback), *Megan Leboutillier*

Facing Codependence, (audiocassette), *Pia Mellody*

Rebuilding: When Your Relationship Ends, (paperback), *Bruce Fisher*

SERENITY PRAYER

God, grant me the serenity
To accept the things I cannot change,
The courage to change the things I can,
And the wisdom to know the diffcrence.

*(AA and other 12-step organizations use the Serenity Prayer
to help recovering people as they attempt to accept their disease,
to take an inventory, to make amends,
and to accept God's will for their lives one day at a time.)*

(Codependent's Version)

God, grant me the serenity
To accept the things I cannot change,
The courage to change the things I can,
And the wisdom to know it is me.

RECOVERY PHILOSOPHY

1. We must be committed to spiritual growth to obtain a peaceful, positive, joyous life.

2. To obtain inner peace we must let go and let God. We cannot control anyone or anything outside of ourselves (including some of the outcomes in our own lives).

3. We must understand and accept there is a power greater than ourselves.

4. We must understand and accept that we have a choice to trust our Higher Power to guide us. If we choose to let our Higher Power guide us, it makes our life more peaceful and serene. If we choose not to, our life becomes burdensome and difficult.

5. We must become honest with our past and present attitudes, feelings, emotions, thoughts, behavior, personality traits and motives, with help from our Higher Power.

6. We must trust at least one other person (a friend or therapist) with all of our emotions and behavior patterns as we become aware of them.

7. We must learn to accept ourselves exactly as we are without denial, hiding, disguising, distorting, or judging that part of ourselves.

8. We must give ourselves time for our emotional growth to catch up with intellectual growth, as long as we are willing to continue to self assess and soul search.

9. We must forgive those who have harmed us in the past, freely and completely. By cleansing our emotions we let go of anger, shame, guilt, grudges and resentments. This will allow us to grow in mind, body and spirit.

10. Most importantly, we must forgive ourselves for the past harm we have caused to ourselves and to others .

11. Once we have admitted and released these wrongs we need to learn to love ourselves.

12. Finally, we must maintain a daily relationship with our Higher Power through prayer and meditation.

THE TWELVE-STEP PROGRAM

Courtesy of Alcoholics Anonymous (AA)

STEP 1: We admit we are powerless over our dependencies and that our lives have become unmanageable.

> We use dependencies to avoid our pain. We live in a fantasy world. We cannot cope with life. Our denial kept us from seeing how powerless and unmanageable our lives had become. Surrender, honesty, willingness are the answers.

STEP 2: We came to believe that a power greater than ourselves could restore us to sanity.

> The insanity is that we continue the same behavior and expect different results. There is a difference between powerless and being helpless. Powerless does not mean hopeless. It means letting go.

STEP 3: We made a decision to turn our will and our lives over to the care of God.

> When we rely on God we begin to trust ourselves, and others. We give him our past, our future, our will, our body, soul & spirit.

STEP 4: We made a searching and fearless moral inventory of ourselves.

> Honesty is the key that breaks the denial of unhealthy behaviors: lying, cheating, stealing, pride, greed, lust, envy, jealousy, gluttony, slothfulness, violence, and perfectionism.

STEP 5: We admitted to God, to ourselves and to another human being the exact nature of our wrongs.

> Confession promotes healing: We are as sick as our secrets. Courage is not the absence of fear but the ability to overcome it.

STEP 6: We were entirely ready to have God remove all these defects of character.

> This is a lifelong process. It is progress, not perfection. A transformation is occurring.

STEP 7: We humbly asked God to remove our shortcomings.

> God uses pain to change us, not to punish us. Now the truth sets us free.

STEP 8: We made a list of all persons we had harmed and became willing to make amends to them all.

> Our willingness is the importance of this step. We are willing to face the damage we caused ourselves and others. We learn to stop blaming others and learn to focus on taking responsibility for ourselves. We have blamed our parents, our relatives, our friends, out teachers, and even God. We put ourselves first on the list to make amends to. We forgive ourselves for our wrongs and we stop punishing ourselves.

STEP 9: We made direct amends to such people whenever possible, except when to do so would injure them or others.

> We have to make amends face to face where possible. Sometimes it may hurt someone to make direct amends, therefore we may write a letter to God asking for forgiveness and healing of the other person. Healing damaged relationships has begun.

STEP 10: We continued to take personal inventory and when we were wrong, promptly admitted it.

> We continue to take inventory of ourselves to assure we keep a clear conscience. We have replaced fear, guilt, shame, isolation, loneliness, anger and other destructive behaviors with gratitude, acceptance, humility, forgiveness, generosity, caring, truth, patience, respect, and humor. We make a gratitude list and add to it daily.

STEP 11: We sought through prayer and meditation to improve our conscious contact with God, as we understand God, praying only for the knowledge of His will for us and the power to carry that out.

> Doing the right thing gives us a sense that what we do is in harmony with the order of all things. Prayer is talking to God. Meditation is listening to God.

STEP 12: Having had a spiritual awakening as a result of these steps, we try to carry this message to others and to practice these principles in all our affairs.

> Just as the prodigal son was restored to his rightful place, God is restoring us to our rightful place. We practice the principles of the steps in every area of our lives. We help others on their exodus from bondage.

THE TWELVE TRADITIONS

Courtesy of Co-Dependents Anonymous (CoDA)
www.codependents.org

1. Our common welfare should come first; personal recovery depends upon CoDA unity.   **2.** For our group purpose there is but one ultimate authority – a loving higher power as expressed to our group conscience. Our leaders are but trusted servants; they do not govern.   **3.** The only requirement for membership in CoDA is a desire for healthy and loving relationships.   **4.** Each group should remain autonomous except in matters affecting other groups or CoDA as a whole.   **5.** Each group has but one primary purpose – to carry its message to other codependents who still suffer. **6.** A CoDA group ought never endorse, finance, or lend the CoDA name to any related facility or outside enterprise, lest problems of money, property and prestige divert us from our primary spiritual aim.   **7.** A CoDA group ought to be fully self-supporting, declining outside contributions.   **8.** CoDependents Anonymous should remain forever non-professional, but our service centers may employ special workers.   **9.** CoDA, as such, ought never be organized; but we may create service boards or committees directly responsible to those they serve.   **10.** CoDA has no opinion on outside issues; hence the CoDA name ought never be drawn into public controversy.   **11.** Our public relations policy is based on attraction rather than promotion; we need always maintain personal anonymity at the level of press, radio, and films.   **12.** Anonymity is the spiritual foundation of all our traditions – ever reminding us to place principles before personalities.

PATTERNS AND CHARACTERISTICS OF CODEPENDENCE

Courtesy of Codependents Anonymous (CoDA)
www.codependents.org

Denial Patterns:

I have difficulty identifying what I am feeling.

I minimize, alter or deny how I truly feel.

I perceive myself as completely unselfish and dedicated to the well being of others.

Low Self Esteem Patterns:

I have difficulty making decisions.

I judge everything I think, say or do harshly, as never "good enough."

I am embarrassed to receive recognition and praise or gifts.

I do not ask others to meet my needs or desires.

I value others' approval of my thinking, feelings and behavior over my own.

I do not perceive myself as a lovable or worthwhile person.

Compliance Patterns:

I compromise my own values and integrity to avoid rejection or others' anger.

I am very sensitive to how others are feeling and feel the same.

I am extremely loyal, remaining in harmful situations too long.

I value others' opinions and feelings more than my own and am afraid to express differing opinions and feelings of my own.

I put aside my own interests and hobbies in order to do what others want.

I accept sex when I want love.

Control Patterns:

I believe most other people are incapable of taking care of themselves.

I attempt to convince others of what they "should" think and how they "truly" feel.

I become resentful when others will not let me help them.

I freely offer others advice and directions without being asked.

I lavish gifts and favors on those I care about.

I use sex to gain approval and acceptance.

I have to be "needed" in order to have a relationship with others.

AFFIRMATIONS

Thoughts to focus on...
to heal yourself and those around you.

Today I let go and let God.

I release all negative thoughts and energy.

Today I am embracing a positive self-image.

I can set realistic boundaries for myself and others.

Today and everyday I love me.

I have unconditional love for others.

I can love someone and still tell them no.

I forgive myself and all others.

Each one reach one, each one teach one.

With my Higher Power, all things are possible.

One day at a time.

I have peace within.

ABOUT THE AUTHORS

Lorraine R. Johnson, Ph.D., L.C.S.W.

My professional counseling career began after receiving an M.S.W. from San Diego State University School of Social Work, my B.A. in social work from San Diego State University, and my Ph.D. in psychology from Crenshaw Christian College and Graduate School. I have been a lecturer for the Africana Studies Department of SDSU since 1995, a social worker for San Diego County Child Protective Services and the San Diego Unified School District, and consultant to numerous public and private sector organizations.

Currently semi-retired, I continue to provide counseling and life coaching in my private practice office in San Diego, California. I specialize in working with entertainers, professional athletes and people who are committed to living a drug-free and codependent-free lifestyle. I also continue to conduct seminars, workshops and public appearances.

I am a widow with three adult male children and five grandchildren. My mother is 80 years old and my grandmother is 99. I am truly blessed they are alive and well and supportive.

I put God first, me second, my elders, children and grandchildren next. My ministry to the world community is an abiding passion. My eldest son Rudy and I are committed to supporting all community programs and activities that promote recovery.

Rudolph A. Johnson III

Currently I am the Vice President/San Diego Convention Center Director, responsible for the management of operational services, client services, administrative support functions, and telecommunication services within the newly-expanded Center.

I previously served as Director of Operations, as well as Assistant Director and had a lead role in managing the Convention Center Expansion Project, which was officially completed in September 2001. I joined the corporation as a Special Projects Manager in 1998 after nine years of service with the City of San Diego.

I received my Bachelor's Degree in Civil Engineering from Texas Southern University and hold a Master's Degree in Public Administration.

To serve my community, I am on the board of directors for Neighborhood House Association and am affiliated with Inroads, the San Diego Urban League, and Pros and Coaches (an anti-drug campaign I created). I was honored to be named to San Diego Metropolitan's 40 Under Forty Honor Roll and to receive the KGTV Channel 10 Leadership Award.

My wife, Sheryl, and I have been married for fourteen years and have two children, Rudy IV (age 11) and Mallory (age 4).

CONTACT THE AUTHORS

Both authors are available
for individual, group, and community
presentations, workshops, seminars, and book signings.

Please contact us at:
1-800-970-3050
(phone and fax)

Email: crackingupthebook@cox.net

Mailing address:
A Piece of Blackberry Pie, Inc.
Cracking Up
P.O. Box 153436
San Diego, CA 92195-3436

Our Love and Blessings for Recovery, Restoration, and Healing,

Dr. "J." (mother) and Rudy (son)

To Order Additional Books

CRACKING UP x _____ at $14.95* = $_____ . _____

CA Sales Tax @ 7.75% = $_____ . _____

Shipping: add $3.00 per book = $_____ . _____

TOTAL = $_____ . _____

To order by FAX: 1-800-970-3050

To order by MAIL:

Please make check payable to: **A Piece of Blackberry Pie, Inc.**

Send your name, phone number, shipping address, and check for
the total amount (including tax and shipping) to:

A Piece of Blackberry Pie, Inc.
Cracking Up
P.O. Box 153436
San Diego, CA 92195-3436

To pay by CREDIT CARD:

Type of card: ☐ **VISA** ☐ MasterCard.

Name as it appears on card: _____

Expiration date: _____ / _____ / _____

Signature: _____

✻ Special price for volume purchases! ✻